Taxcafe.co.uk Tax Guides

The Investor's Tax Bible

How to Slash Your Taxes When You Trade or Invest in Shares, Bonds, Options & CFDs

By Lee Hadnum LLB ACA CTA

Important Legal Notices:

Taxcafe®
TAX GUIDE - "The Investor's Tax Bible: How to Slash Your Taxes When You Trade or Invest in Shares, Bonds, Options & CFDs"

Published by:
Taxcafe UK Limited
67 Milton Road
Kirkcaldy KY1 1TL
Tel: (0044) 01592 560081
Email: team@taxcafe.co.uk

Seventh Edition, May 2009

ISBN 978-1-904608-93-6

Disclaimer

1. Please note that this tax guide is intended as general guidance only for individual readers and does NOT constitute accountancy, tax, investment or other professional advice. Taxcafe UK Limited and the author accept no responsibility or liability for loss which may arise from reliance on information contained in this tax guide.

2. Please note that tax legislation, the law and practices by government and regulatory authorities (eg HM Revenue and Customs) are constantly changing. We therefore recommend that for accountancy, tax, investment or other professional advice, you consult a suitably qualified accountant, tax specialist, independent financial adviser, or other professional adviser. Please also note that your personal circumstances may vary from the general examples given in this tax guide and your professional adviser will be able to give specific advice based on your personal circumstances.

3. This tax guide covers UK taxation only and any references to 'tax' or 'taxation' in this tax guide, unless the contrary is expressly stated, refers to UK taxation only. Please note that references to the 'UK' do not include the Channel Islands or the Isle of Man. Foreign tax implications are beyond the scope of this tax guide.

4. Whilst in an effort to be helpful, this tax guide may refer to general guidance on matters other than UK taxation. Taxcafe UK Limited and the author are not experts in these matters and do not accept any responsibility or liability for loss which may arise from reliance on such information contained in this tax guide.

5. Please note that Taxcafe UK Limited has relied wholly upon the expertise of the author in the preparation of the content of this tax guide. The author is not an employee of Taxcafe UK Limited but has been selected by Taxcafe UK Limited using reasonable care and skill to write the content of this tax guide.

Other Taxcafe.co.uk guides by Lee Hadnum

Using a Company to Save Tax

The World's Best Tax Havens

Non-Resident & Offshore Tax Planning

Selling your Business

Tax Saving Tactics for Non-Doms

About The Author

Lee Hadnum is a key member of the Taxcafe team. Apart from authoring a number of our tax guides, he also provides personalised tax advice through our popular Question & Answer Service, a role he carries out with a great deal of enthusiasm and professionalism.

Lee is a rarity among tax advisers having both legal AND chartered accountancy qualifications. After qualifying as a prize winner in the Institute of Chartered Accountants entrance exams, he went on to become a Chartered Tax Adviser (CTA).

Having worked in Ernst & Young's tax department for a number of years, Lee decided to start his own tax consulting firm, specialising in capital gains tax, inheritance tax and business tax planning. He now provides online guidance and unique tax planning reports for financial market traders and investors at:

www.traderstaxclub.co.uk

Whenever he has spare time he enjoys DIY, walking and travelling.

Contents

Introduction

This guide takes an in-depth look at how tax affects stock market traders and investors. The focus throughout is on translating complex tax concepts into plain English and providing guidance, wherever possible, on how to cut your tax bill.

The guide contains numerous examples to illustrate every key point. There is also a tremendous amount of unique 'number crunching', which provides fascinating results and will help you pay less tax.

The capital gains tax regime has changed pretty radically for share investors who sell shares after 5 April 2008. There are therefore essentially two sets of rules that apply – one for disposals on or before 5 April 2008, and another set of rules for disposals after 5 April 2008.

In this book we shall focus on the new rules for disposals after 5 April 2008. However, we also realise that there may be one or two readers who have sold shares before 6 April 2008 and are looking for guidance on how to calculate the gain. We've therefore included a separate chapter on disposals before 6 April 2008 which explains the old rules.

Turning to the individual chapters, in Chapter 1 we summarise all the taxes you face as a stock market investor and pinpoint which ones are the most important. Chapter 2 illustrates good versus bad tax planning and why trying to save tax should never be your main priority.

The main focus of this guide is capital gains tax because this is the tax that affects investors most... and offers the most scope for constructive tax planning. In Chapter 3 we provide a quick introduction to how capital gains tax is calculated.

In Chapter 4 we take a more detailed look at each component of the capital gains tax calculation: Proceeds, acquisition cost, the complex share matching rules, what expenditure you can and cannot deduct, tax reliefs and the annual capital gains tax exemption. We then examine how the final tax bill is calculated.

Chapter 5 explains the rules for disposals prior to 6 April 2008.

1

In the next three chapters we examine some specific cases. In Chapter 6 we explain how unit trust and other fund investors calculate capital gains tax and some of the special tax rules that apply to these investments. Chapter 7 takes a closer look at calculating tax on rights issues and takeovers. Chapter 8 shows how gains from options and warrants are taxed, as well as taking a quick look at CFDs.

Once you've calculated your capital gains tax you may have to complete the special CGT pages of the tax return. Chapter 9 explains when and how to do this.

The next 10 chapters cover capital gains tax planning: In Chapter 10 you'll learn how to make the most of your annual exemption by making frequent share disposals, Chapter 11 shows how married couples can split their gains and achieve a lower tax bill, and Chapter 12 looks at how assets can be gifted to children so that they can make use of their annual CGT exemptions.

In Chapter 13 we then explain what strategies you should follow to make the most of your losses, Chapter 14 explains the tax benefits of ISAs and how you should use them to obtain the maximum tax relief, and Chapter 15 covers spread betting and compares this activity with normal share trading.

Chapter 16 looks at why unit trusts are a fantastic tax shelter for investors who have already made use of their annual capital gains tax exemptions, and Chapter 17 covers the two main tax shelters available to UK share investors: venture capital trusts and enterprise investment schemes.

Chapter 18 takes an in-depth look at the tax benefits of investing in equities compared with property and finally in Chapter 19 we look at non-resident and offshore tax planning.

In Chapter 20 the focus changes to gilts and corporate bonds and we examine their place in your investment portfolio and *how* you should invest in these important assets to ensure that your after-tax returns are beating inflation.

In Chapter 21 we examine the income tax treatment of dividends and how they compare with income from other investments. We also look at ways married couples can split their income... and all the traps to avoid.

Chapter 22 looks at some of the tax changes announced in the 2009 Budget that will come into force in April 2010, including the new 50% super tax and the withdrawal of personal allowances for those earning over £100,000.

Chapter 23 is all about inheritance tax and how this impacts on stock market investing and the kind of planning you can undertake to minimise the eventual tax bill.

Many share investors ask whether it is better to be taxed as a 'trader' or an 'investor'. Chapter 24 answers this question pretty definitively.

Chapter 25 weighs up all the tax benefits and drawbacks of setting up your own company to trade in shares.

Finally, Chapter 26 explains how share clubs are taxed.

Throughout the guide we use examples and some of them relate to tax years. Remember the tax year always starts on April 6 and ends the next year on April 5. We also use a number of abbreviations, the most common ones being CGT (capital gains tax), IHT (inheritance tax) and HMRC (HM Revenue and Customs).

You will also notice that we often talk about 'share investors' when in fact we are referring to 'financial asset investors', which doesn't have quite the same ring to it! The latter includes bond investors, unit trust investors etc. There are specific tax rules that relate to these investments and which we highlight but much of the guide applies to all financial assets, not just shares.

Finally, remember there is a BIG difference between what stock market enthusiasts mean by the terms 'share trader' and 'share investor' and what the taxman takes these words to mean. The taxman has a number of guidelines as to what constitutes trading and investment, the latter being subject to capital gains tax, the former being subject to income tax. Even very active buyers and sellers of financial assets are usually 'investors' in the taxman's eyes and subject to capital gains tax. In Chapter 24 all of this will be explained.

Chapter 1

What Taxes Do Stock Market Investors Pay?

There are a whole variety of taxes that you could end up paying if you are a share trader or investor. The most important ones are:

Income Tax

Individuals pay income tax on any income they receive from shares or other securities.

How much tax you pay depends on how much income you earn during the tax year:

- Interest is taxed at 10%, 20% or 40%.
- Dividends are taxed at 10% or 32.5%, although the 'effective' tax rates will be either 0% or 25%.

In addition, it should be noted that any trading income is subject to income tax, although it would be taxed at either 20% or 40%.

In the 2009 Budget the Chancellor announced a new 'supertax' which will apply to anyone earning over £150,000 per tax year from April 2010.

We'll look at the impact of this shortly, however in essence, interest or trading income above £150,000 will be taxed at 50%, whereas dividends above £150,000 will be taxed at an effective rate of 36.1%.

In most cases profits made from selling shares are subject to capital gains tax. However, if the taxman classes you as a share trader your profits will be taxed as income.

Chapter 24 examines in detail the tax implications of being classified as a share trader.

Capital Gains Tax (CGT)

For most investors this is the most important tax to consider and it is examined in considerable detail throughout this guide.

Capital gains tax is usually payable on any profit you make when you sell an asset. More precisely, tax is payable on the 'chargeable gain', which is the amount left over after you have deducted a variety of reliefs and allowances.

The rate of CGT for disposals after 5 April 2008 is now fixed at 18%. For higher rate taxpayers this now means that there are considerable advantages to being taxed on capital gains rather than income as there is a 22% tax saving in 2009/10.

Although capital gains tax is the tax most feared by investors it is also the one that offers the most opportunities for constructive tax planning.

Stamp Duty

Individuals and companies have to pay stamp duty when they buy most shares or other securities.

The rate for shares is fixed at 0.5%.

There's not much you can do to avoid stamp duty (except join the campaign to have it abolished!). However, share investors are much luckier than property investors who often end up paying 3-4% on their investments.

Corporation Tax

A UK resident company pays corporation tax on its worldwide income, profits and gains. It does not pay income tax or capital gains tax.

To calculate a company's tax bill, its total income and capital gains are simply added together and subjected to corporation tax.

The effective rates of corporation tax vary from (currently) 21% to 29.75%, depending on the level of the company's profits.

The reason we mention this tax here is that, in Chapter 25, we will be taking a detailed look at the pros and cons of starting your own company to trade shares.

Inheritance Tax (IHT)

Any shares owned at the date of an individual's death will ordinarily be included within the estate for inheritance tax purposes, although there are certain reliefs available.

Where it applies, IHT is charged at 40% on the value of the estate exceeding the nil rate band (currently £325,000 for the 2009/2010 tax year).

There are special provisions for transfers of shares (or other assets) to trusts or companies in which case an immediate inheritance tax charge can arise, irrespective of the fact that the person making the gift has not yet died.

Companies aren't liable for inheritance tax although in exceptional circumstances certain dealings by companies can result in shareholders paying tax. Inheritance tax is covered in greater detail in Chapter 23.

National Insurance

National insurance would only be relevant if:

- You take on an employee to assist you in your share dealing activities. In this case, class 1 primary and secondary contributions would be payable (by the employee and the employer).

- You are classed as a share trader. In this case class 2 and 4 contributions would be payable by you, as with any self-employed individual.

- You establish a company and decide to pay yourself a salary. In this case class 1 contributions have to be paid.

National insurance is covered in more detail in chapters 24 and 25, where we take a detailed look at share trading and the pros and cons of using a company. For the vast majority of share investors national insurance is not an issue.

Value Added Tax (VAT)

Almost every share investor or trader will end up paying VAT, for example when you pay for software, website subscriptions or other electronic information. For example, if you bought the electronic version of this tax guide from our website you will have paid VAT! However, if you bought the printed edition you will not have paid any VAT because printed books are 'zero-rated'.

In the vast majority of cases there is nothing you can do about VAT. In the unlikely event that you are VAT registered the tax you pay can be recovered in full.

Summary

As a share investor or trader you are likely to pay a wide variety of taxes: income tax, capital gains tax, stamp duty, VAT and inheritance tax.

The most important tax, without doubt, is capital gains tax. If gains on disposal are large your tax bill could also represent a significant sum. However, as we will see, there is plenty you can do about it.

Chapter 2

Good vs Bad Tax Planning

The primary aim of anyone buying or selling shares or other securities is to make money. This may sound obvious but many assets such as property, classic cars, rare stamps and fine art, are often also bought for pleasure.

With shares it's much more cut and dried. Most serious investors enjoy researching what companies to buy and tracking their progress. Ultimately, however, the real buzz comes from making a profit.

Because making money is the only thing that counts and when you consider that, in the worst case scenario, you could be losing 18% of your profits to the taxman, tax planning should always feature high on your agenda.

Take the example of Warren and Gordon. Let's say Warren buys some shares for £5,000 and sells them for £15,000 but ends up paying 18% tax. He will end up with £13,200.

If Gordon only manages to sell his shares for £14,750 but, through careful planning, ends up paying 10% tax, he will end up with £13,775. Warren may be a better stock picker but Gordon is surely the better investor.

This example is simplistic but the point is clear. Good tax planning can have a significant effect on your after-tax returns.

The critical point is this:

It's not big profits you're after but big *after-tax profits*.

While tax planning is a critical part of the process, there is good tax planning and bad tax planning. Saving tax should never be you primary consideration. If it were, everyone would invest solely in venture capital trusts. These are possibly the best tax shelters available but unfortunately they're also incredibly risky.

What's so great about paying zero per cent tax on your profits if you have no profits in the first place? We call this spending £1 to save 18p in tax.

Here are some typical examples of BAD tax planning:

- Using up your annual ISA allowance even though you're not confident shares will do well this year.

- Postponing a sale of shares until the new tax year, only to find the markets plummeting in early April.

- Selling shares to make use of your annual capital gains tax exemption only to see them soar in value before you've had a chance to reinvest.

- Investing in a venture capital trust to make use of the generous income tax relief, only to find that the shares in the fund fall by more than 30% before you're legally allowed to sell them.

- If you're not domiciled in the UK, investing in US shares because the profits will not be immediately taxed in the UK, only to find that the US market underperforms the UK market.

- Topping up your pension contributions, only to find that you need the cash to pay your children's school fees.

- Becoming taxed as a share trader so that you can claim extra tax deductions, only to find that your expenses do not exceed your forfeited annual capital gains tax exemption.

- Reinvesting all your profits after the end of the tax year, even though some may be owing to the taxman.

- And, worst of all, gifting assets to your spouse who later on runs off to Barbados with your stockbroker!

In each case the investor has his eye on saving tax instead of maximising his total after-tax profits.

Throughout this guide our focus will be on realistic tax saving strategies that do not jeopardise the primary objective: to make successful investments!

Chapter 3

Capital Gains Tax: a Brief Snapshot

Although many accountants would have you believe otherwise, the basic capital gains tax calculation is pretty straightforward especially for disposals after 5 April 2008.

Once you sell shares you have what are called 'disposal proceeds'. Subtracting the purchase cost of the shares you end up with what most investors would describe as their profit.

However, this is not the amount that gets taxed. From your profit you can deduct certain expenses, such as stamp duty and stockbroker's fees.

There is then the potential to offset some reliefs depending on the shares in question and the circumstances of the disposal.

From this you can deduct your annual capital gains tax exemption. Whatever's left gets taxed at 18%.

A typical capital gains tax calculation is summarised in Table 1.

Table 1: Typical CGT Calculation

Proceeds	X
Less:	
Acquisition cost	(X)
Deductible expenses	(X)
Reliefs	(X)
Chargeable gain	**X**
Less:	
Annual exemption	(X)
Taxable gain	X

Example

Aaron sells shares for £16,000 in December 2009. He bought them for £5,000 in December 2006. His profit is therefore £11,000. From this we subtract deductible expenditure of, say, £75 (representing stamp duty and broker's commission). He can offset the annual CGT exemption of £10,100 and deducting this leaves a taxable gain of £825. He'll then pay CGT at 18%, with his tax bill being £148.50.

Of course, matters aren't always this simple. Every step of the typical CGT calculation outlined above has a variety of 'ifs', 'buts' and 'maybes'. In the next chapter we'll analyse the CGT calculation in more detail before getting stuck into some constructive tax planning from Chapter 10 onwards.

Effective CGT Rates

However, before we go on to examine the capital gains tax calculation in detail it's worth pointing out that CGT is often not as onerous as most investors expect.

The new 18% flat rate of CGT has significantly reduced the tax burden on disposals and when you take into account the annual CGT exemption, which protects a further £10,100 *per person*, your 'effective tax rate' will usually be much lower than 18%.

By 'effective tax rate' we mean the total tax expressed as a percentage of your profits.

The capital gains tax rate may be 18% but thanks to the various deductions allowed you will only pay 18% on the 'chargeable gain'. The chargeable gain is often much lower than the actual profit.

For example, in Table 2 we illustrate some effective tax rates for taxpayers with different levels of profit. The first column is for married couples (who enjoy two CGT reliefs), the second column is for single investors. These figures are calculated after taking account of the annual CGT exemptions and assume that the 18% flat rate of CGT applies. The table makes interesting reading because it shows that even if you earn tens of thousands of pounds of investment profits, you may end up paying tax at rates much lower than 18% - without resorting to any fancy tax planning!

TABLE 2: EFFECTIVE CGT RATES

Profits	Married Couples	Single Investors
£10,000	0	0
£20,000	0	9
£30,000	6	12
£40,000	9	13
£50,000	11	14
£60,000	12	15
£70,000	13	15
£80,000	13	16
£90,000	14	16
£100,000	14	16
£120,000	15	16
£150,000	16	17
£200,000	16	17

What Assets are Subject to CGT?

It's also important to point out that not all assets fall into the capital gains tax net. The table below lists some of the more popular types of investment, along with their capital gains tax treatment.

Subject to CGT?

UK shares	Yes
Overseas shares	Yes
Unit trusts	Yes
Enterprise investment scheme shares	No
Venture capital trusts	No
Gilts	No
Corporate bonds	Usually No
Warrants/options	Yes
CFDs	Yes
Futures	Yes
Gold coins	Yes
Spread betting	No

Venture capital trust profits and spread betting profits are completely tax free, as are capital gains from gilts and most corporate bonds. Shares in unquoted companies that qualify under the Enterprise Investment Scheme are also free of capital gains tax. Hedge fund profits are usually subject to income tax.

We'll analyze the special tax rules applying to some of these investments later in the guide.

And of course certain 'investment wrappers' (to use that horrible term) protect most of the above assets from capital gains tax. The best known one is the ISA which is examined in detail in Chapter 14.

Who Pays Capital Gains Tax?

Most investors are subject to capital gains tax when they sell shares or other assets. However, if the taxman classes you as a trader you will instead pay income tax on your profits. The pros and cons of being classed as a share trader are examined in Chapter 24.

You also have to be UK resident and UK 'ordinarily resident' to pay UK capital gains tax. We'll take a close look at non-resident tax planning issues in Chapter 19.

Share trader status is not easy to acquire (and usually not very desirable!) and becoming non-resident does not appeal to the vast majority of investors (especially if it's done for tax reasons only) so the vast majority of those buying and selling shares will pay capital gains tax on their investment profits.

This is why we focus so much of our attention on CGT in this guide.

Chapter 4

Capital Gains Tax: Detailed Calculations

In this chapter we take a detailed look at each component of the capital gains tax calculation:

- Disposal proceeds
- Acquisition cost, including the share matching rules.
- Tax deductible expenses
- Entrepreneurs Relief
- The annual CGT exemption

We'll then explain how the final tax bill is calculated and how to complete the capital gains tax pages of your tax return. After that we'll take a brief look at some CGT 'special cases': unit trust and OEIC profits, options and warrants and rights issues and takeovers.

What are Your Proceeds?

In the vast majority of cases the disposal proceeds are simply the cash received when the shares or other assets are sold.

However, if you sell your shares to a 'connected person' for less than they're worth or if the transaction is not at 'arm's length', the disposal proceeds will be the true market value of the shares, rather than the payment you receive (which may be significantly less).

Connected persons include:

- Your spouse
- Your children or remoter descendants
- Your parents or remoter ancestors
- Your brothers and sisters and their spouses
- Your spouse's relatives, eg brothers, sisters or parents.
- Business partners

Although your husband or wife is a connected person, it's critical to point out that there is no capital gains tax payable if you transfer assets to your spouse or civil partner (more about this in Chapter 11).

Example

Johnny decides to give his shares in No Profit plc to his brother as a birthday present. The quoted price of the shares on the date of the gift is £1.25 per share. The gift will represent a disposal by Johnny and capital gains tax will be payable, based on proceeds of £1.25 per share.

There are other situations where the transaction might not be at arm's length and market value will be substituted for the actual disposal proceeds, for example:

- Transfers between unmarried couples, and
- Sales of shares to employees

In these circumstances the onus of proof that the transaction was not at arm's length rests with Revenue and Customs.

The market value of quoted shares is, of course, easy to determine. When *unquoted* shares are involved, it is likely that Revenue's share valuation division will negotiate an acceptable value with you, looking at factors such as the company's financial performance, equivalent price earnings ratios and dividend yields and whether you are a controlling shareholder.

What is Your Acquisition Cost?

If you bought shares in a company on only one occasion, it's easy to identify the acquisition cost for the capital gains tax calculation: it's simply the amount you paid for the shares.

If you bought the shares prior to 31 March 1982, the so-called MV82 rule comes into play. In these circumstances, the acquisition cost is deemed to be the value of the shares on 31 March 1982. This provision effectively eliminates tax on any profit earned before 31 March 1982.

If you've bought shares in the same company and of the same class on a number of different occasions, the calculation gets more tricky.

In these instances the 'share identification' or 'share matching' rules come into play.

Share Matching Rules

These rules have been designed in large part to prevent investors from making the most of the annual capital gains tax exemption. Nevertheless it is still possible to beat the system as we will see later.

The matching rules used to be significantly more complex than they are now, but the changes to the capital gains tax regime have greatly simplified them.

For disposals after 5 April 2008 if you've bought shares in the same company more than once, you are treated as selling shares in the following order:

- Shares bought on the same day.
- Shares bought in the 30 days following the sale.
- Shares in the 'New 1985 pool'.

The Same Day Rule

Let's say you bought 11,000 shares in a company for £1 each two years ago and they've since doubled in price to £2. You may want to hold onto these shares for many years... but you also don't want to waste your annual CGT exemption. So you realize a tax-free profit of £10,100 by selling 10,100 shares. You then buy the shares back immediately before the price changes.

Unfortunately the taxman will not let you get away with this. The sale and purchase that took place on the same day will be viewed as a single transaction. In other words, the shares you sold are *not* the ones you purchased two years ago that are showing a big profit. In the taxman's eyes the shares you sold are the ones you bought back on the same day.

There will be no capital gain showing on these, so you won't be able to make use of your capital gains tax allowance. You will still be left with 11,000 shares with a base cost of £1 and a 100% profit on which you will have to pay tax when sold.

The 30 Day Rule

Instead of buying the shares back on the same day, you wait a week. That's not good enough either. From the taxman's standpoint the shares you sold are the ones you bought seven days later, again with possibly little or no capital gain to offset against your annual CGT allowance. This rule applies if you buy the same shares at any time within 30 days.

The 30 day rule works on the 'First In First Out' (FIFO) basis. To illustrate what this means, let's say you buy and sell shares in the same company on the following dates:

- 1 June   Buy 1,000 shares for £20,000
- 10 June   Sell 1,000 shares for £24,000
- 20 June   Buy 1,000 shares for £24,000
- 25 June   Sell 1,000 shares for £30,000
- 28 June   Buy 1,000 shares for £30,000

The disposal on June 10 will be matched with the first purchase in the *next* 30 days. The first purchase was on June 20. In other words, the proceeds for the CGT calculation will be £24,000 and the acquisition cost will be £24,000 resulting in no taxable gain.

Similarly, the disposal on June 25 will be matched with the purchase on June 28, resulting in no taxable gain.

This may sound like a good thing because no tax is payable. However, the investor is still left with 1,000 shares which originally cost £20,000 and are now worth £30,000.

When these are sold there could be a tax charge unless they are disposed of gradually to take advantage of the annual CGT exemption.

The New 1985 Pool (also known as the S104 Holding)

This new pool means that all share purchases of the same type in the same company are treated as a single pool, growing or diminishing as shares are acquired and disposed of.

The allowable cost on a disposal will therefore essentially represent a pro rating of the total cost of all the shares (in other words, the average cost of the shares is treated as the purchase price).

Before the 2008 changes, the 1985 pool operated in this way but it could not contain shares acquired before 6 April 1982 or after 5 April 1998. The new pool has now been widened to include all shares except for those acquired on the same day or in the next 30 days of disposal. The value of the pool is adjusted each time you sell some shares.

Example

Bert acquired shares in X plc as follows:

15 May 2001	*5,000*	*£10,000*
27 June 2007	*10,000*	*£25,000*
9 September 2008	*10,000*	*£30,000*

He then sold 15,000 shares in October 2009 for £60,000. Under the pre April 2008 rules his disposal would be matched as follows:

10,000 in September 2008	*£30,000*
5,000 in June 2007	*£12,500*

The total base cost to be used when working out the capital gain would be £42,500.

Under the new rules the pool would contain all of the shares as follows:

Total cost	*£65,000*
Number of shares	*25,000*
Average cost per share	*£2.60*

On a disposal of 15,000 shares the base cost would be £39,000 (15,000 x £2.60)

This is a much simpler method of calculating gains and means that investors will simply add the cost of shares including any incidental costs such as stamp duty etc to the pool for calculating gains.

Summary

Remember you only have to worry about the share matching rules if you make *multiple purchases* in the same company. These rules will then need to be applied to identify which acquisition costs are to be used when you dispose of some shares.

If you make just one purchase of a company's shares, these rules will not apply and you will simply use the one acquisition cost when calculating your gain.

Even if they do apply, the same-day and next 30-day rules are pretty straightforward and for the rest of the purchases you are simply effectively calculating the average cost based on your total shareholding.

Deductible Expenses

Once you've subtracted the acquisition cost from the disposal proceeds, you can claim costs directly related to the acquisition and disposal of the shares.

By and large, the only costs you can claim are:

- Stamp duty
- Stockbroker's dealing costs

You can also claim fees in connection with valuing shares, although this would only be of use to investors in unquoted companies.

Be warned that HMRC is likely to contest any attempt to claim any extra expenses.

For example, you cannot claim a deduction with respect to:

- Subscriptions to periodicals or websites
- Investment software
- Stockbroker's advisory fees
- Tax adviser's fees

Share traders, on the other hand, can claim an enormous number of expenses. We take a closer look at share trading in Chapter 24.

Entrepreneurs Relief

As part of the reform of the capital gains tax system, taper relief which used to apply to disposals of all assets including shares has now been withdrawn.

On the upside, the rate of capital gains tax has been reduced to a fixed rate of 18%.

This will make most higher-rate taxpayers much better off. Unless they were investing in shares that qualified as 'business assets' such as unquoted shares in trading companies (including companies quoted on the Alternative Investment Market) taper relief could reduce their capital gains tax charge at best to 24%.

The new 18% flat rate of CGT will therefore be a tremendous benefit for most share investors.

It's worthwhile mentioning that there is also a new relief – Entrepreneurs Relief – that has been introduced from 6 April 2008.

Although it will not apply to most share investors it is worthwhile bearing in mind.

Where it applies it will reduce the effective rate of capital gains tax from 18% to 10% on the first £1 million of capital gains (this is a lifetime limit).

In the context of shares though it will only apply where the company that you hold the shares in is a trading company (or holding company of a trading group) and is also classed as your 'personal company'.

In order to satisfy the requirement of being your personal company you would need to own at least 5% of the shares (and voting rights) and be an employee or officer for at least 1 year prior to the disposal.

The 5% shareholding requirement puts this out of reach of most stock market investors although there may be circumstances where it could apply.

The Annual CGT Exemption

Investors who make full use of the annual exemption can protect profits of up to £10,100 per year from tax. Furthermore, because the annual exemption is *per person*, if an asset is jointly owned by a husband and wife, two annual exemptions will be available. This gives a couple a total deduction of £20,200 every year. Over a period of 10 years that's worth as much as £36,360 in tax savings! It is important to note that:

- The annual exemption is either used or lost in a tax year. It is not possible to carry forward all or part of the annual exemption to the following tax year.

- The annual exemption is offset against the *total* gains arising in a tax year, and not against each gain arising on an asset disposal.

- The annual exemption is the last relief deducted when calculating your capital gains tax liability.

The Tax Rate

Once you've subtracted the cost of your shares from the sale proceeds and then deducted all allowable expenses and the annual CGT exemption, what's left is taxed at 18%.

Note that if you have no other income, your personal allowance of £6,475 can NOT be offset against your taxable capital gains. For example, if your spouse earns no other income but earns a capital gain of £1,000 above the annual exemption, this will be fully taxed at 18%.

Of course most people earn other income as well in which case their gains are classed as separate from their other income.

Example

In the 2009/10 tax year, Steven earns a salary of £35,000 and taxable gains of £12,500 from selling shares. His tax calculation is as follows:

Salary	*£35,000*
Less:	
Personal allowance	*£6,475*
	£28,525

Tax on salary

28,525 @ 20%	*£5,705*

Income tax   **£5,705**

Next we calculate Steven's capital gains tax liability. This is simply charged at 18% irrespective of the fact that his gains would actually push his total income and gains into the 40% income tax band.

Tax on share disposal

£12,500 @ 18%	*£2,250*
Capital gains tax	***£2,250***

Summary

The capital gains tax calculation can be summarised as follows:

- First determine the 'proceeds', in most cases the cash value of the shares sold. If the sale is to a 'connected' person (eg a family member) the taxman will replace the selling price with the market value.

- Next deduct the acquisition cost. This is easy to calculate if you have only bought the share once – it's simply the price you paid. If you have bought the shares on more than one occasion you have to use the share matching rules.

- Shares sold are matched first with any bought on the same day. If none, you have to match the shares sold with purchases over the next 30 days on the FIFO basis. If none, you match the shares sold with the average cost as calculated in the New 1985 Pool.

- Once you've determined the acquisition cost of the shares you can deduct a limited amount of expenses: stockbroker's fees and stamp duty being the main allowable costs.

- You'll then be deducting the annual CGT exemption and applying the 18% rate of CGT.

Chapter 5

Disposals Before 6 April 2008

Although the capital gains tax rules have changed pretty radically for disposals after 5 April 2008 it's well worth including the 'old' rules in this book. Not least because many readers may have made disposals in tax year 2007/2008 and will be interested in how both previous and future disposals will be taxed.

The capital gains tax calculation on a 2007/2008 disposal would look like this:

Typical CGT Calculation

Proceeds	X
Less:	
Acquisition cost	(X)
Deductible expenses	(X)
Indexation allowance	(X)
Taper relief	(X)
Chargeable gain	**X**
Less:	
Annual exemption	(X)
Taxable gain	X

The main differences from the new rules are that you can potentially claim indexation relief and taper relief and that the tax rates are up to 40%. We'll look at these in a minute but first it's important to look at how the share matching rules differed.

Share Matching Rules

If you've bought shares in the same company more than once, you are treated as selling shares in the following order:

- Shares bought on the same day.
- Shares bought in the 30 days following the sale.
- Shares bought after April 5 1998, taking the most recent acquisitions first.
- Shares in the '1985 pool', known as the 'section 104 holding'.
- Shares in the '1982 pool'.
- Shares held on April 6 1965.

The 'same day' rule and the 'following 30 days' rule are exactly the same as under the current rules. The main difference is in relation to the shares that don't fall into these categories.

Other Shares Bought Since April 5 1998:

The LIFO Rule

This rule applies to all other shares bought on and after April 6 1998. Let's say you bought 10,000 shares for £1 each on April 5 2001 and a further 10,000 at the same price on April 6 2006. It's now April 5 2008, the shares have risen to £3 so you decide to take some profits and sell half your holding. Which shares have you sold? The ones bought in 2001 or the one bought in 2006?

This is extremely important from a tax-planning perspective. You've just realised a £20,000 profit so your annual CGT exemption will not be sufficient to eradicate your tax charge. The shares bought in 2001 will qualify for 25% taper relief because they've been held for seven years, the shares bought in 2006 do not qualify for any taper relief.

Unfortunately the taxman uses the 'Last In First Out' (LIFO) basis, which means it's your newest acquisitions which are sold first, ie the ones which qualify for the least taper relief.

Example

Chloe buys shares in Rich plc on the following dates:

	Number	**Cost £**
• 6 May 2001	2,000	2,000
• 28 March 2006	2,000	3,000
• 15 November 2007	2,000	3,500
• 6 December 2007	2,000	4,000

In total she bought 8,000 shares for £12,500. On December 6 2007 she sells 7,000 shares for £17,500 (she also bought 2,000 shares on December 6 but late in the afternoon, after another major price rise, she decides to drastically reduce her holding).

Here's how the shares sold are matched with shares purchased to determine cost for the capital gains tax calculation:

- *Same day (6 December purchase)*   *2,000 shares*
- *LIFO (15 November purchase)*   *2,000 shares*
- *LIFO (28 March purchase)*   *2,000 shares*
- *LIFO (6 May purchase)*   *1,000 shares*

The acquisition cost used in the CGT calculation will be:

- *Same day (6 December purchase)*   *£4,000*
- *LIFO (15 November purchase)*   *£3,500*
- *LIFO (28 March purchase)*   *£3,000*
- *LIFO (6 May purchase)*   *£1,000*

The total acquisition cost for the CGT calculation is £11,500.

What about shares purchased before April 6 1998? Here calculating the acquisition cost gets a bit more complex if there were multiple purchases prior to that date.

The '1985 Pool' or 'Section 104 Holding'

Shares of the same type bought between April 6 1982 and April 5 1998 are pooled for tax purposes and the average cost of the shares is treated as the purchase price.

This is what's known as the '1985 pool' or the 'section 104 holding'.

The total value of the pool is simply the total cost of the holdings plus indexation from the dates of purchase until April 5 1998.

The value of the pool is adjusted each time you sell some shares.

The steps you have to take to work out the gain when you sell shares in the pool are best illustrated by means of an example.

Example

Kirsty bought and sold shares in Marks plc on the following dates:

		Number	**Cost £**
•	*6 June 1990*	*1,000*	*12,000*
•	*6 August 1995*	*2,600*	*6,000*

The first step is to calculate indexation from the date of acquisition until April 1998 as follows:

6 June 1990 Shares

The Retail Prices Index rose by 28.3% between June 1990 and April 1998. Multiplying by the cost of the shares, £12,000, you get the indexation relief:

28.3% x £12,000 = £3,396

6 August 1995 Shares

The Retail Prices Index rose by 8.5% between August 1995 and April 1998. Multiplying by the cost of the shares, £6,000, you get the indexation relief:

8.5% x £6,000 = £510

The £3,396 and £510 are added to the £18,000 cost of the shares to obtain the 1985 pool (it's called the 1985 pool because it also applies to earlier acquisitions).

The total value of the 1985 pool is £21,906.

Now let's say Kirsty sells 5,000 of her 7,400 shares to pay for her daughter's wedding. The cost of these shares (known as the 'indexed cost') used in the capital gains tax calculation is:

5,000/7,400 x £21,906 = £14,801

The '1982 Pool'

Shares bought between April 7 1965 and April 5 1982 are kept in a separate pool, called the '1982 holding'. Again, the cost of the shares in the pool is added together and each share is treated as if acquired at the same average cost.

Finally shares held at April 6 1965 are treated as separate acquisitions and not pooled.

Indexation Relief

The Indexation allowance is designed to give a measure of relief for the effects of inflation. Here are the main points you need to know:

- It applies to shares bought between March 1982 and April 1998.

- It only applies to pre-April 1998 purchases. After April 1998, taper relief kicks in.

- The amount of relief you get depends on the increase in the Retail Prices Index between the purchase date and April 1998.

- The percentage rise in the RPI is multiplied by the cost of the shares – the resulting number is your indexation allowance.

- Indexation relief can be used to reduce or eliminate a capital gain to zero. It cannot be used to create a loss.

Example

Pablo bought shares for £10,000 in July 1990. He sells them for £20,000 in June 2007. The amount of Indexation Relief he gets depends on how much the Retail Prices Index (RPI) rose between July 1990 and April 1998.

The RPI in July 1990 was 126.8 and the RPI in April 1998 was 162.6. Therefore the index rose by 28.2%. Pablo's indexation relief is £2,820:

£10,000 x 28.2% = £2,820

In other words his taxable gain is reduced by £2,820. The gain remaining after indexation relief has been deducted is usually referred to as the 'indexed gain' by accountants.

A list of indexation percentages covering all investment time periods is contained in Appendix B.

Taper Relief

Disposals before 6 April 2008 qualify for taper relief.

The amount of taper relief you qualify for depends not only on how long you have held an asset but the *nature* of the asset. There are two types of taper relief: non-business asset taper relief (most share investments qualify for this relief) and its more generous cousin, business-asset taper relief (only certain types of shares qualify).

We'll focus on business assets first for the simple reason that, if an asset doesn't meet the 'business asset' definition, it automatically qualifies for non-business asset taper relief.

Business Assets

Since 6 April 2000, the following shares are classified as business assets:

- Shares in unquoted trading companies and unquoted holding companies of a trading group.

- Shares quoted on the Alternative Investment Market (AIM).

- Shares in quoted trading companies and quoted holding companies, if the shareholder is an employee of the company or can exercise at least 5% of the voting rights in the company.

- Shares in non-trading companies if the shareholder is an employee of the company and does not own more than 10% of the shares.

For periods *before* 6 April 2000, the following types of shareholding are classified as business assets:

- Shareholdings in trading companies where the shareholder owns at least 5% of the voting rights and was a full-time working director or employee, or

- Shareholdings where the shareholder owns at least 25% of the voting rights.

There are therefore two definitions of business asset, depending on whether the shares were owned prior to April 6 2000. It is possible that certain holdings will be regarded as non-business assets up to 5 April 2000 and business assets thereafter.

Example 1

Jack purchased a 2% shareholding in an unquoted trading company on 7 September 1998. As he did not work for the company from 7 September 1998 until 5 April 2000, the shareholding will be treated as a non-business asset. From 6 April 2000 the shareholding will be regarded as a business asset.

Example 2

Peter was a full time director of ABC Ltd, an unquoted trading company. He held 7% of the share capital and voting rights from the incorporation of the company in June 1995. He disposed of his shares in May 2007. Peter's shareholding will be treated as a business asset from 6 April 1998, the date taper relief was introduced.

Business Asset Taper Relief Rates

So how much is Business Asset Taper Relief worth? For disposals after April 5 2002 the following rates apply:

- For assets held less than 1 year: **Nil**
- For assets held for 1 year but less than 2 years: **50%**
- For assets held for 2 years or more: **75%**

Note that by 'one year' and 'two years' we are not referring to tax years. In other words, to qualify for 75% taper relief you only have to hold the asset for more than 24 months – not two complete tax years (which could be significantly more than 24 months).

So how do these rates work in practice? The basic principle is: if you qualify for 50% taper relief then 50% of your profits (after deducting indexation relief and incidental costs) are tax free. The other 50% is taxed but may be reduced by your annual CGT exemption.

Example

Peter purchased £10,000 of AIM shares on May 1 2004. He sold them at the end of June 2007 for £18,000. His CGT calculation is as follows:

Proceeds	*£18,000*
Less: Cost	*£10,000*
Less: Taper Relief	
75% of £8,000	*£6,000*
Less: Annual CGT Exemption	*£2,000*
Tax Payable	*NIL*

Note that the annual capital gains tax exemption (£9,200 for tax year 2007/2008) can only be used to reduce the gain to zero – not to create a loss.

Non-Business Assets

Any assets not meeting the above 'business asset' definition will be classed as non-business assets and qualify for the following rates of taper relief:

- For assets held for less than 3 years: **Nil**
- For assets held for 3 years but less than 4 years: **5%**
- For assets held for 4 years but less than 5 years: **10%**
- For assets held for 5 years but less than 6 years: **15%**
- For assets held for 6 years but less than 7 years: **20%**
- For assets held for 7 years but less than 8 years: **25%**
- For assets held for 8 years but less than 9 years: **30%**
- For assets held for 9 years but less than 10 years: **35%**
- For assets held for 10 years or longer: **40%**

Most shares and unit trust investments qualify for this type of taper relief. Once again please note that 'years' refers to 12-month periods, not tax years. This type of taper relief is much less generous than its business asset cousin. For starters you have to own assets for more than three years just to qualify and it increases very gradually until you have held the asset for 10 years.

There is a special rule for disposals of non-business assets: If the shares were owned on 17 March 1998, an additional one 'bonus year' of ownership is added.

Example 1

Paul bought shares worth £20,000 in a FTSE 100 company on May 1 2002. He sold them at the end of June 2007 for £40,000. His CGT calculation is as follows:

Proceeds	*£40,000*
Less: Cost	*£20,000*
Less: Taper Relief	
15% of £20,000	*£3,000*
Less: CGT exemption	*£9,200*
Taxable Gain	*£7,800*

Rate of CGT

The rate of CGT will depend on how much income you have earned during the tax year, as any chargeable gain will be added to your other income and taxed at your marginal rate of tax. Capital gains are taxed at either 10%, 20% or 40%.

Chapter 6

Unit Trusts, OEICs and Investment Trusts

Unit trusts, investment trusts and OEICs are treated in much the same way as other share investments for capital gains tax purposes. In other words, the rules outlined above can be used to calculate your capital gains tax.

There are, however, a number of quirks and capital gains tax calculations can be quite tricky. In this chapter we will explain in plain English how you calculate your capital gains tax if you sell a unit trust, investment trust or OEIC holding.

The Nature of the Asset

The first point to note is that if you invest in a unit trust the *nature* of the underlying assets is ignored. For example, if you invest in a gilt fund your capital gains are not exempt from tax, unlike direct investors who pay no CGT when they sell. This is an important point to remember. Unit trusts and other funds offer tremendous benefits but they may result in you qualifying for less tax relief or having profits taxed that would otherwise be exempt.

Accumulation Units vs Income Units

Unit trust investors who want to reinvest their annual income distributions can choose between Accumulation units or Income Units. If you hold accumulation units you do not receive income distributions. Instead the income is reinvested automatically, raising the value of your existing units.

In contrast, if you invest in income units and reinvest your income, these are treated as new purchases.

This used to be an important distinction in terms of maximising taper relief but now that taper relief has been withdrawn the main benefit of accumulation units is that they are generally easier to handle when completing your tax return.

Umbrella Funds

If you invest in an umbrella fund which allows you to switch from one fund to another, such switches are treated as disposals and will give rise to capital gains tax.

Monthly Savings Schemes

Many funds offer a monthly saving scheme and this is an attractive way to invest gradually in the stock market. However, it also means you have lots of separate asset purchases which simply means that you'll need to keep careful records of the purchases to ensure you correctly calculate the acquisition cost.

When you come to sell your units you have to first apply the share matching rules to identify which units have been sold (see Chapter 4 for the details).

The basic rule, remember, is that the 'New 1985 Pool' now applies to provide an averaged cost basis.

Once you've identified the base cost you can then calculate your capital gain.

Example

Ricky starts investing £500 on the 25th of each month in a unit trust savings scheme in January 2005. We'll assume for simplicity that there are no dividend payments. In December 2007, after three years, he stops contributing.

His investments are summarised in Table 3. On March 31 2010 he decides to put a £15,000 deposit on an investment property. So he sells 5,180 units which are now worth £2.90 each.

Following the new rules that apply for disposals after 5 April 2008, Ricky will firstly make sure there were no acquisitions on the day of the disposal or in the following 30 days.

Because there are none, Ricky will calculate his pool for all of his share purchases. He therefore has a total shareholding of 13,663 units with an acquisition cost of £18,000.

As he has sold 5,180 units his base cost would be:

5,180/13,663 x £18,000 = £6,824

His capital gain would be calculated as:

Proceeds (£2.90 x 5,180) *£15,022*

Less: Acquisition cost *(£6,824)*

Capital Gain *£8,198*

If Ricky has no other taxable gains this amount will be easily covered by his annual CGT exemption.

Table 3: Ricky's Monthly Investments

Month	Price £	Units	Cost
January 2005	1	500	500
February 2005	1.02	490	500
March 2005	1.04	481	500
April 2005	1.06	472	500
May 2005	1.08	463	500
June 2005	1.1	455	500
July 2005	1.12	446	500
August 2005	1.14	439	500
September 2005	1.16	431	500
October 2005	1.18	424	500
November 2005	1.2	417	500
December 2005	1.22	410	500
January 2006	1.24	403	500
February 2006	1.26	397	500
March 2006	1.28	391	500
April 2006	1.3	385	500
May 2006	1.32	379	500
June 2006	1.34	373	500
July 2006	1.36	368	500
August 2006	1.38	362	500
September 2006	1.4	357	500
October 2006	1.42	352	500
November 2006	1.44	347	500
December 2006	1.46	342	500
January 2007	1.48	338	500
February 2007	1.5	333	500
March 2007	1.52	329	500
April 2007	1.54	325	500
May 2007	1.56	321	500
June 2007	1.58	316	500
July 2007	1.6	313	500
August 2007	1.62	309	500
September 2007	1.64	305	500
October 2007	1.66	301	500
November 2007	1.68	298	500
December 2007	1.7	294	500
Total		**13,663**	**18,000**

Chapter 7

Takeovers and Rights Issues

Takeovers

Let's assume you buy 1,000 shares in Gordon plc for £1 each. The company does well and attracts a takeover bid from Monster plc. Monster plc could either make a cash offer for your shares or offer you shares in Monster plc in exchange.

A cash payment will result in capital gains tax having to be paid. If Monster offers you £10 per share, you will have a gain of £9,000 (before deducting any reliefs).

If Monster offers you shares in its own company in exchange, there are provisions that can apply so that there is deemed to be no taxable gain and the new shares are deemed to have been acquired on the same date as the Gordon plc shares. The new shares are treated as 'standing in the shoes' of the old shares.

There are certain Revenue and Customs conditions that must be met but which are not worth examining in any detail here.

Rights Issues

If a shareholder decides to take up a rights issue no taxable gain arises. In many cases, however, shareholders accept cash payments instead. A sale of rights is classed as a part disposal for capital gains tax purposes. The tax calculation is based on the increase in value of a proportion of the original shareholding.

Under normal circumstances, the proceeds will be the amount received for the sale of the rights.

However, the sale of rights is not treated as a disposal if the proceeds are 'small'. 'Small' is not defined in the legislation. However, HMRC states that it will treat proceeds as small if they are equal to or less than 5 per cent of the value of the underlying shares (at the date of the rights issue), or £3,000, whichever is the greatest of these figures.

When these conditions are met, it is referred to as a small part disposal and in most cases the proceeds are subtracted from the base cost which essentially transfers any gain arising from the sale of the rights to the year in which the shares creating the rights are sold.

The small part disposal rules can therefore defer capital gains tax until a future disposal of the shares, giving a valuable cash flow benefit, as you will already have received cash when you sold your rights.

Calculating the Cost of the Rights

As with any asset, in order to calculate any gain arising, we need to be able to identify the cost of the asset disposed of. The cost of the rights is taken to be a proportion of the base cost of the shares creating the rights. When all the rights are sold, this proportion is given by the following formula:

Base cost × sale proceeds /(current value of original shares + sale proceeds)

When only some of the rights are disposed of, and some are taken up, the denominator (the part in brackets) in the above formula changes to:

(Current value of original shares + value of rights taken up + sale proceeds)

For the majority of small investors, the sale of rights will not result in tax having to be paid due to the effects of the small part disposal rules and the application of the annual CGT exemption.

If you don't think you will have other chargeable gains in the tax year you sell your rights, the small part disposal rules can be 'disapplied' so as to ensure that a chargeable gain arises which will be covered by the annual exemption.

Chapter 8

Options and Warrants

Options are used to speculate on share price movements or hedge portfolios against share price falls. Either way, the profits are normally subject to capital gains tax. The same goes for warrants.

I say 'normally' because it is possible to be classed as a *trader* in options, just as it is possible to be classed as a trader in shares. In these instances your profits will be subject to income tax. (See Chapter 24 for more on the tax treatment of traders.)

In this chapter we'll examine the capital gains tax implications of buying and selling options and warrants as it's these tax rules that will apply most often.

If you're buying and selling options frequently, the normal share matching rules will apply, provided the options are of the same 'class' and 'series' (in other words, provided they have the same expiry date and exercise price).

The main difference between the ordinary CGT rules and the rules which apply to warrants and traded options is that the abandonment of the option is treated as a disposal.

This means that the grantee of the option (that is, the person who buys the option) will obtain an allowable loss for capital gains tax purposes if the option is simply allowed to expire.

If you decide to exercise an option or warrant, its cost is added to the exercise price of the shares to determine the base cost for the CGT calculation.

Example

David buys 5,000 warrants in ABC plc, which give him the right to purchase one share per warrant at a price of £3.00 within the next three years. He pays a premium of 10p per warrant.

If he subsequently exercises the warrants, his total base cost will be £15,500 (the cost of the warrants and the cost of the shares).

David subsequently sells the 5,000 shares for £5.00 each.
The CGT calculation will be as follows:

Proceeds	*£25,000*
Less: Cost	*£15,500*
Gain	*£9,500*

Of course, the actual option or warrant may never be exercised if you sell it for a profit before the expiry date. This would be a simple disposal for CGT purposes and the gain (before CGT reliefs) would be the uplift in value from the price paid to proceeds received.

Tax Planning

Options and warrants can be put to a number of uses:

Crystallisation of Losses

Let's assume Bob holds 1,000 shares in Slump plc. He purchased them at a price of £4.40, but the share price has now decreased to £1.40. He is therefore sitting on a capital loss of £3,000 (£4.40 - £1.40 x 1,000).

He has made other share disposals during the tax year and has crystallised gains of £13,100.

To avoid paying any tax, it may be desirable for Bob to dispose of the Slump plc shares and offset his loss against his gains, with the remaining gain being reduced by the annual capital gains tax exemption.

However, maybe Bob is reluctant to dispose of his Slump plc shares as he is confident they are going to enjoy a rebound shortly.

What should he do?

He could sell the Slump plc shares, thereby crystallising his loss for tax purposes but take out an option to buy the shares. If the price subsequently rises he will still benefit by holding a position in Slump but will have reduced his CGT liability by utilizing his loss.

Using the Annual CGT Exemption

Options and warrants allow you to take profits to utilise your annual CGT exemption (worth up to £1,818 per year in saved tax) and avoid falling foul of the taxman's share matching rules. Remember the share matching rules prevent you from selling shares and buying them back for 30 days.

However, there's nothing HMRC can do if, instead of buying back the shares, you buy options instead. Using options (and spread betting contracts for that matter) you can make sure that you retain your exposure to the underlying asset and make maximum use of the annual CGT exemption.

Delaying the Date of Disposal

Options can be used to delay the date of disposal of a shareholding. Postponing the disposal date provides three key tax benefits:

- You could end up with an extra 12 months to pay capital gains tax, if you manage to push your disposal into the next tax year.

- It can help you make the most of capital losses.

- If you have used your annual exemption for the current tax year but don't expect to do so for the next tax year it can allow you to delay the disposal date to utilise the additional annual exemption.

Example

Denis owns 20,000 shares in Dosh plc. They were acquired in May 2003 for £20,000. Denis decides to sell them for £50,000 in February 2010.

The tax calculation will be as follows:

Proceeds	*£50,000*
Less:	
Cost	*£20,000*
CGT allowance	*£10,100*
Taxable Gain	*£19,900*
Tax @ 18%	*£3,582*
After-tax proceeds	*£46,418*

However Denis is expecting to incur a capital loss of £10,000 in the following tax year. He may therefore want to hold onto the shares until after 5 April 2010. If he believes the price of Dosh shares will drop if he holds them until after April, one possibility would be to obtain put options for £2.80 over 20,000 Dosh plc shares at a premium of 0.15p each.

Let's say the value of the shares has decreased to £45,000 in June 2010 and Denis decides to exercise his option. His gain will be calculated as follows:

Proceeds (£2.8 x 20,000)	*£56,000*
Less:	
Original cost	*£20,000*
Cost of option	*£3,000*
Capital loss	*£10,000*
CGT exemption	*£10,100*
Taxable Gain	*£12,900*
Tax @ 18%	*£2,322*
After-tax profits	*£53,678*

Note that in this case the investor's after-tax profits have increased. He has been able to take advantage of the falling price, the capital loss and the tax payment date has been put back from 31 January 2011 to 31 January 2012. This is an extra 12 months that the CGT will be in his bank or invested and making him more money.

Options and the CGT Matching Rules

We've looked at how the matching rules operate when you sell shares, allowing you to determine the correct base cost. The same rules that apply to shares also apply to options.

Generally traded options are on one of three possible expiry cycles:

- January, April, July, October
- February, May, August, November
- March, June, September, December.

Therefore, at any one time there are equity options available with three possible expiry dates. When a new equity option is introduced it is allocated to one of the three cycles.

All options of the same type (ie put or call) relating to the same share are called a class. All options of the same class with the same expiry date and exercise price form a series. For capital gains tax purposes options of the same series will be subject to the share matching rules.

As we've seen, there is a definite order in which acquisitions should be treated. So when you sell options you should look at your holding of options of the same series and match the disposals with:

- Options acquired on the date of disposal
- Options acquired in the 30 days following the date of disposal
- Options acquired before the disposal (ie the new pool)

Example

Bert acquired a £10.00 June call option in X plc as follows:

15 April	*1,000*	*£1,000*
27 May	*10,000*	*£25,000*
29 May	*10,000*	*£30,000*

He then sold 15,000 options for £60,000.

Under the matching rules the pool would contain all of the options as follows:

Number of options   21,000
Cost   £56,000

On a disposal of 15,000 shares the base cost would be £40,000 (ie 15,000/21,000 x £56,000).

Contracts for Difference (CFDs)

A CFD is a method of investing in shares that looks to mirror the benefits of direct ownership while eliminating many of the disadvantages. In particular, CFDs allow for margin payments which means you can invest without paying the full market price of the shares upfront.

They also allow you to benefit from any dividends the company pays during your period of 'ownership' and, unlike shares, CFDs are not subject to stamp duty.

In terms of tax, CFDs are subject to capital gains tax so any losses can be offset against other gains made during the tax year – for example, gains on share disposals.

There are a number of uses for CFDs although the tax implications are closely linked to your particular trading strategy.

One use is to sidestep the provisions that prevent 'bed and breakfasting' of shares. As we know, these apply where shares are sold one day and bought back the next in order to crystallize a loss or use the annual CGT exemption.

HMRC prevents this by stating that any repurchase of the shares in the next 30 days will be matched with the disposal, effectively meaning that the shares are deemed not to be sold at all. However, many investors use CFDs to circumvent this rule.

Repurchasing shares in the form of a CFD allows you to maintain a position in the company during the 30 day period, and you can then repurchase without having lost out on any growth and without the bed and breakfast anti-avoidance rules applying.

Example

Elliott owns shares that are standing at a small gain, for example £5,000, or even at a loss. Prior to the end of the tax year he could dispose of the shares and crystallize the loss or gain. If the shares are showing a gain he could eliminate any tax bill by offsetting his annual exemption. If he can repurchase the shares he will have secured a tax-free uplift in the base cost of the shares.

Elliott then purchases a CFD for the same number of shares. After 31 days he sells the CFD and repurchases the ordinary shares. By using CFDs he will have maintained a position in the shares and won't be any better or worse off if the shares rise or fall in value. For example, if the shares slump then the loss on the CFD trade is offset by the cheaper price he will pay for the shares when they're bought again.

Investors can also use a CFD to hedge against price falls and this short selling is a useful way of managing your liability for capital gains tax. In particular, you can sell CFDs against an existing holding allowing you to control the time at which you crystallize capital gains or losses. This can also be useful for ensuring correct offset of losses and utilization of the annual exemption.

The Tax Benefit of CFDs Over Shares

Most investors knows that CFDs are free of stamp duty. This in itself can result in a sizeable saving where you are investing in contacts with a substantial value.

This is not the only tax benefit of CFDs. To see exactly how good they are you need to look at the alternative, which is a direct investment in the underlying shares (or a currency or commodity).

If you purchase the underlying asset directly the chances are you'll be subject to capital gains tax when you sell it. As such you'll be taxed at 18% on any capital gain. Any dividends received would be subject to income tax at your marginal rate of income tax. So if you're a higher rate taxpayer the effective rate of income tax would currently be 25%.

The only expenses that you would be able to deduct would be the acquisition cost of the shares and any incidental costs of buying and selling – essentially stamp duty and dealing costs.

If you borrowed to invest in the shares there would be no tax deduction for any interest that you incurred. Unless you were taxed as a financial trader this interest paid by you would therefore not qualify for tax relief.

What if You Were Treated as a Trader?

If you were a taxed as a trader you would qualify for tax relief on the interest paid but your profits would be taxed at your marginal income tax rate.

Again, if you're a higher rate taxpayer this would be 40%. Dividends would still be taxed at an effective 25%. So you might get the benefit of the interest deduction but your tax rate would go up substantially.

CFD Investors

Now let's take a look at the position for CFD investors. The whole of the net gain is subject to capital gains tax. This means that you would also benefit from:

- A capital gains tax deduction for interest charged by the CFD provider.

- Dividends subject to CGT and not income tax.

You are still able to deduct commission, as would a share investor, but the additional interest deduction would not be available to a share investor. This potentially saves you tax at 18% on your interest costs.

Similarly the dividends are rolled up as part of the gain and taxed at 18% and not 25%.

Of course, this doesn't take account of the different rates etc that CFD providers charge but, other things being equal, you would expect a CFD investor to have higher after-tax returns than a direct investor.

Chapter 9

How to Complete Your Tax Return

Now that we've looked at the rules for calculating capital gains and losses and examined how to take advantage of the many reliefs on offer, it's time to turn our attention to completing the capital gains tax pages of your tax return.

But first it's important to point out that you may not need to declare anything on your tax return.

Firstly, transfers to spouses, which are completely tax free, do not have to be declared.

Secondly, if your gains are within the annual tax-free limit (currently £10,100) AND the total sales proceeds are within the 'notification limit' (currently £40,400) you do not have to declare anything.

The notification limit is simply the annual capital gains tax exemption multiplied by four.

So if you sell shares showing a gain of £8,000 and the total value of the shares is £40,000, the taxman doesn't have to be told.

(By the way, when we say 'gains' we mean taxable profits before taking into account the annual CGT exemption.)

If your gains OR proceeds exceed these limits you need to complete the CGT portion of your tax return. Even if your gains from share disposals are nil, you still need to complete the CGT pages if the total sales proceeds exceeds the £40,400 notification limit.

If you incur capital *losses* during the year you do not have to report these to Revenue and Customs unless the disposal value exceeds the notification limit. In practice, you should always declare losses so that they can offset gains in future tax years.

If you are non-UK resident and not ordinarily resident, any gains will be exempt and the capital gains tax pages do not need to be completed (subject to the tax anti-avoidance rules).

If you are claiming reliefs such as rollover relief or gift relief you have to ensure that full details of your disposals are included in your tax return.

And finally, if in any doubt, it's better to disclose than fail to disclose. Failure to report information could see your return being classed as completed 'negligently'. As such, the taxman could raise a discovery assessment any time for up to six years. By notifying Revenue and Customs of your disposals, they usually cannot look back into your affairs further than two years.

Details of your gains and losses are provided in the capital gains summary pages – two pages in total. These are not automatically provided with the basic tax return but can be downloaded here: www.hmrc.gov.uk/forms/sa108.pdf

If you do not automatically receive a tax return from HMRC you can download one here: www.hmrc.gov.uk/forms/sa100.pdf

The capital gains summary pages contain five sections:

- A summary of all gains and losses from all types of assets
- Listed shares and other securities
- Unlisted shares and securities
- Property and other assets
- Other information

The tax return for the tax year 2009/2010 will not be released until 2010 and therefore the return that we will explain in this chapter will be the tax return CGT pages for 2008/2009.

On the form itself you provide a summary of your capital gains and losses but you must also provide supporting calculations to back up your figures.

Summary of Your Enclosed Computations

In the first section (see below) you provide a summary of all your gains and losses from sales of all assets (shares, property etc):

Summary of your enclosed computations

You **must** enclose your computations, as well as filling in the boxes – read page CGN 9 of the *notes*.

3 Total gains in the year, before losses £ [ ] · 0 0	**10** Losses available to be carried forward to later years £ [ ] · 0 0	
4 Total losses of the year – *enter '0' if there are none* £ [ ] · 0 0	**11** Losses used against an earlier year's gain (special circumstances apply – *read the notes on page CGN 11*) £ [ ] · 0 0	
5 Losses brought forward and used in the year £ [ ] · 0 0	**12** Losses used against income – *amount claimed against 2008-09 income* £ [ ] · 0 0	
6 Total gains, after losses but before the annual exempt amount £ [ ] · 0 0	**13** Losses used against income – *amount claimed against 2007-08 income* £ [ ] · 0 0	
7 Annual exempt amount £ [ ] · 0 0	**14** Income losses of 2008-09 set against gains £ [ ] · 0 0	
8 Net chargeable gains (box 6 minus box 7) – *but if box 7 is more than box 6, leave blank* £ [ ] · 0 0	**15** Entrepreneurs' relief – *read the notes on pages CGN 7 and CGN 8* £ [ ] · 0 0	
9 Additional liability in respect of non-resident or dual resident trusts £ [ ] · 0 0		

Box 3 – Total gains in the year before losses
Here you will enter your total capital gains for the year from all assets sold before losses. These are your *taxable* gains, after deducting all expenses and reliefs you are entitled to, but before deducting the annual exempt amount (£10,100 in 2009/10, £9,600 in 2008/9).

Box 4 – Total losses in the year
Here you enter the capital losses you incurred during the tax year on all asset disposals.

Box 5 – Total losses brought forward
This box is for any losses from previous tax years that are brought forward to offset against the current year's capital gains.

Remember that brought forward capital losses are only used to reduce the remaining gain to £10,100 – the amount of the annual exemption (£9,600 for 2008/9).

Box 6 – Total gains after losses
You simply offset the capital gains in box 3 against any losses in boxes 4 and 5.

Box 7 – Annual exemption
For the 2009/10 tax year the number in this box is £10,100 (£9,600 for the 2008/9 tax year), unless you're a non-dom claiming the remittance basis (in which case you will not be entitled to offset the annual CGT exemption).

Box 8 – Net chargeable gains
This is simply box 6 minus box 7.

Box 10 – Losses to carry forward
Any surplus losses from the current year or previous years will be carried forward for offset against future capital gains. These will be entered in this box.

The above are the boxes most commonly used. The rest of the boxes (ie box 9 and boxes 11-13) will be used by very few readers.

If you have any income tax losses and make a claim for these to be offset against capital gains you may need to enter these in box 14. These could be trading losses or losses from furnished holiday lettings.

Box 15 would also be completed if you are entitled to Entrepreneurs Relief (most stock market investors would not qualify).

Listed Shares and Securities

If you've sold listed shares and other securities (which, as a reader of this book, you probably have), you also have to complete the second section: "Listed shares and securities" .

Listed shares and securities

Box 16 - Number of disposals
This is the number of times you have sold shares. For example if you sold 1,000 Standard Life shares in May and 1,000 BP shares in October, the number in this box would be "2".

Box 17 - Disposal proceeds
Your disposal proceeds are the total value of all the shares you have sold, before deducting costs.

Box 18 – Allowable costs
For share investors this includes both your buying and selling costs (normally stamp duty and commission) and the original purchase price of the shares.

Box 19- Gains in the year, before losses
Just your capital gains go in this box – in other words, capital gains before any losses are offset (either current year or previous year losses).

Box 20 - Claims or Elections
If you're making a claim for any of the CGT reliefs (aside from Entrepreneurs Relief) you would tick this box.

Typical claims will include:

- Rollover relief
- Gift relief
- Negligible value claims
- EIS relief

Box 21 - Estimates
You will tick this box if an estimate or valuation was used for the

shares. This would be most likely to occur if you transferred the shares to a connected party.

Deadline

As a general rule, if you have chargeable gains or losses you will need to complete a tax return for the year in question. If you don't input details of your capital losses on your tax return, you have five years and 10 months from the end of the tax year in which to claim the loss.

For example, a capital loss incurred in tax year 2003/2004 would need to be claimed (in a tax return) by 31 January 2010.

Changes in the 2007 Budget affected the filing date for tax years 2007/2008 onwards. The new provisions mean that your filing date will depend on whether you file your return online or not. If you file online your tax return along with any associated tax will need to be submitted by 31st January following the tax year in question.

However, if you want to submit a paper return you'll need to submit it by 31st October. For the 2008/2009 tax year you'll therefore need to file a paper return by 31st October 2009.

Capital gains tax is always payable by 31st January following the end of the tax year. Therefore, for the tax year running from 6th April 2008 to 5th April 2009, the CGT is due to be paid by 31st January 2010.

Chapter 10

Making the Most of Your Annual CGT Exemption

Regular Annual Disposals – How Do You Do It?

Because the annual capital gains tax exemption is worth up to £1,818 in saved tax each year (£3,636 if you're married), it makes sense to sell shares that are showing a profit so that the exemption is not wasted.

The problem is you may still want to hold on to the shares because you expect them to rise in value.

It's no longer possible to sell your shares and buy them back immediately (so-called bed and breakfasting). You have to wait 30 days to avoid the anti-avoidance rules (see Chapter 4 on share matching). By then, of course, it may be too late and the shares may have risen in value.

However, there are still ways of getting around the share matching rules:

Bed & Spousing

If you're married one solution is to get your spouse to buy back the shares – also known as 'bed and spousing'.

Example

Bob sells shares with profits of £10,100 in the 2009/2010 tax year and transfers the funds to his wife, Betty, who buys the same shares immediately. Bob's profits are completely tax free and Betty now owns the same shares and can benefit from any price increase.

Note that with any transaction between husband and wife care must be taken to ensure that absolute ownership does pass to the wife and it is not a 'sham arrangement'.

Note this strategy will not work if the shares are owned jointly. For example, Bob and Betty may have bought the shares in joint names so that when the time came to sell they could make use of two CGT exemptions, instead of just Bob's.

Bed & ISA

An alternative method of avoiding the share matching rules is to repurchase shares through an ISA. The ISA is regarded as the new legal owner in the eyes of the taxman and therefore you can avoid the 30-day matching rule.

Example

Pat has 10,000 shares in Bucks plc. They were originally acquired for £4,000, and have now increased in value to £7,000. He still has his annual CGT exemption for the 2009/2010 tax year available on April 3rd 2010. He decides to give himself a tax-free uplift in the base cost of his shares by disposing of his entire holding. The gain of £3,000 is covered by his annual exemption and he can then buy the shares again through an ISA.

If he did not use the ISA, he would have had to wait 30 days before repurchasing the shares in order to avoid the matching rules. During this period the shares might have increased in value and Pat would have lost out.

Bed & Options or Bed & Spread Bet

There's nothing stopping you from selling your shares to take advantage of your CGT exemption and covering your position for 30 days using either options or other derivatives or a spread betting contract. Naturally you have to know what you're doing but this tactic would completely avoid the share matching rules.

Profits from spread betting are completely tax free, profits from derivatives trades are generally subject to CGT so you would have to do your number crunching and see if the exercise is worthwhile.

Similar Shares or Funds

Let's say you've already used up your ISA allowance, your investments are owned jointly with your spouse and you don't fancy using derivatives or other complicated financial assets. However, you do have some handsome profits and would like to use up your annual CGT exemption.

One option is to simply purchase similar shares or invest in a similar fund. This is, of course, the second-best option but may well be worth considering.

Example

Kathy and Dave jointly own shares in Copper Top plc worth £20,000 which were originally purchased two years ago for £10,000. They sell now and potentially save £1,800 in future capital gains tax (£10,000 profit x 18% tax = £1,800). They decide to invest in Copper Bottom plc for 30 days so they can maintain exposure to the copper market even though this company is not as attractive.

During the 30-day period Copper Top rises 10% and Copper Bottom rises just 5%. In other words, they have lost out on a 5% rise, worth £1,000 (£20,000 Copper Top holding x 5% = £1,000). However, they've saved £1,800 tax so they're still better off.

Whether this strategy is worth following depends critically on whether your profits are large when expressed as a percentage of your total holding. If so, it may well be worth selling now.

It also depends critically on how important to you losing the annual CGT exemption is. You have to decide whether losing this year's CGT allowance will result in a much larger tax bill later on.

This strategy is arguably most suited to unit trust investors, in particular investors in index trackers who can easily substitute one fund for another without losing out on performance.

Sit it Out for 30 Days

Another alternative is to simply sell your investment, wait for 30 days and then reinvest. Here you have to weigh up your tax savings with the potential for the share price to rise.

Example

Kathy and Dave jointly own shares in a company worth £20,000 which were originally purchased two years ago for £10,000. They sell now and, using their CGT exemptions potentially save £1,800 in future capital gains tax. They decide to wait 30 days before buying again to comply with the 30-day rule. In that time the shares jump 5%. In other words, Kathy and Dave have saved £1,800 but lost out on £1,000 of profits. They're still well ahead, however, and the sale was arguably worthwhile.

Whatever you do it's important not to let the tax tail wag the investment dog!

Costs versus Tax Savings

If you sell shares or units in a fund purely to make use of your annual CGT exemption you still have to reinvest the proceeds. This will inevitably result in charges. In the case of shares there is brokerage, stamp duty and of course the bid/offer spread.

With unit trusts the costs are potentially far higher. For example many unit trusts levy an initial charge of as much as 5%. In these circumstances, where investment costs are quite high, it is essential to weigh up the costs versus the potential tax savings.

Remember, making use of your £10,100 annual exemption means taking *profits* of £10,100, which may mean selling a considerably far greater amount of shares if your returns are quite low.

Example

John has £100,000 invested in a unit trust. Over the course of the tax year he makes a profit of £10,100 and decides to sell his entire holding to make use of his annual CGT exemption. Doing so he saves himself

£1,818 in tax (£10,100 x 18%). He then decides to reinvest in a different fund (to avoid the 30-day rule).

Because he has a large amount of capital he is able to get a discount on the initial charge and ends up paying 3% instead of the normal 5%. However he still ends up paying £3,303 in charges, completely wiping out his tax savings.

This is an extreme example but proves an important point: selling shares for tax reasons alone can be dangerous especially when costs are high or you have to dispose of a large block of shares to use all your CGT exemption.

Chapter 11

How Your Spouse Can Help Cut Your Tax Bill

It's one of the most important tax breaks available and you should always think of ways of exploiting it:

Spouses can transfer shares or other assets to each other without paying any capital gains tax.

There are several reasons why you may wish to transfer assets to a spouse. Firstly, if the assets generate income it makes sense for the spouse with the lowest tax rate to earn it (see Chapter 21 on income splitting with your spouse).

Secondly, if you want to sell some shares it makes sense to hold shares jointly so both spouses can exploit the annual capital gains tax exemption.

Making the Most of Losses

The tax break for inter-spouse transfers can also be used to make the most of capital losses.

Example

Joe is married to Jenna. Joe has shares in ABC plc standing at a gain of £25,000 (after all reliefs). Jenna has a capital loss of £35,000 from a disposal of a number of her shares a number of years ago.

In order to eliminate his CGT charge, Joe could simply transfer the shares to Jenna. Jenna could then dispose of the shares and offset her old capital loss against the current year's capital gain.

The Legal Stuff

Note that this rule applies to married couples and civil partners who are living together for at least part of the tax year in question. The Civil Partnerships Act 2004 gives civil partners the same tax treatment as married couples as of 5 December 2005.

For tax purposes a husband and wife, or civil partners, are treated as 'living together' unless they are:

- Separated under a court order or separation deed, or

- Separated and circumstances point to it being permanent.

Example

Pete and Petra decide to separate in August 2009. The decree absolute is awarded in September 2011. Pete and Petra can make tax-free transfers for the whole of the 2009/2010 tax year even though they are not 'living together' from August 2009. (Although it's anyone's guess why they would want to transfer assets to each other!)

For the 2010/2011 tax year they will not have been living together during any part of the tax year and therefore tax-free transfers cannot be made. Instead, it is likely that Pete and Petra will be regarded as 'connected parties' and capital gains tax will be payable based on the full market value of the assets transferred.

For periods after the decree absolute is awarded, the normal CGT rules will apply.

Watch Out For Income Tax

The transfer of shares to a spouse applies not only for capital gains tax purposes but for income tax and inheritance tax too.

Example

Jack is married to Jill. Jack is a basic-rate taxpayer and Jill is a higher rate taxpayer. Jack owns shares in XYZ plc and decides to transfer half his shareholding to his wife in order that two annual exemptions can be utilised when the shares are eventually sold.

The problem with this is that if XYZ plc has a high dividend yield any dividends will be taxed in Jack and Jill's hands equally, although Jack will pay no income tax as he is a basic-rate taxpayer, and Jill will pay an effective 25% in 2009/2010. Therefore if they both received £5,000 of dividends, Jill would pay £1,250 income tax. If the shares had been retained by Jack no income tax would be payable.

So in this case joint ownership confers a capital gains tax benefit but an income tax penalty.

HMRC Election

Where assets are held jointly by spouses the general rule is that Revenue and Customs will treat you each as being entitled to 50% of the income. This is irrespective of the actual ownership, and could work to your advantage. For example, if a higher earning spouse actually enjoys 90% of the income, he could benefit from being taxed on just 50% of the income.

If you wish to split income in any other proportion, you are permitted to submit an election to HMRC stating what proportion you each own. Therefore if you wanted to be taxed on 90% of the dividends with your wife taxed on the remaining 10%, you could make this election and HMRC would accept it. (The necessary form is available from: www.hmrc.gov.uk/forms/form17.pdf)

Note that this proportion would then usually be taken as the ownership for CGT purposes and care would need to be taken when considering whether to make the election.

There were changes to the application of these rules in the 2004 Budget but only as regards shares in close companies (these are companies that are controlled by the directors or only a few shareholders – eg family companies). For these companies the assumption of a 50:50 split is not made, and the income would be taxed on the actual entitlement.

Transfers and CGT

In order to minimise any adverse income tax consequences you may think it's best to simply transfer shares immediately prior to a disposal.

However, transferring shares to a spouse to minimise CGT needs to be approached with caution. It is advisable that the final disposal does not take place just after the interspouse transfer. It is possible that anti-avoidance provisions could be invoked by HMRC.

Frequently, husband and wife transfers are made with little supporting documentation. As a minimum, a transfer of the beneficial interest should be undertaken, and in this case supporting evidence should include a signed and dated deed of gift.

For added certainty, should HMRC enquire into the matter, you may decide to amend the share certificates showing the joint ownership of the shares.

The transfer should be a reality and not merely an artificial exercise which HMRC could argue is a 'sham'.

The spouse receiving the shares should therefore, for all intents and purposes, be the owner of the shares and have the normal rights of ownership. For example, on the eventual disposal of the shares the funds should not be immediately channelled back to the original spouse holding the shares.

Chapter 12

How Your Children Can Help Cut Your Tax Bill

It's possible to gift your children shares or cash to buy shares and any profits will be taxed in *their* hands, allowing full use to be made of their annual capital gains tax exemptions. Children of *all ages* qualify for an annual CGT exemption.

There are, however, traps to watch out for when gifting shares or other assets to children:

- When you transfer the shares you will have to pay capital gains tax because transfers to children are classed as 'disposals' for CGT purposes. So caution has to be exercised when transferring shares which are already showing handsome profits or if you've already made use of your own CGT exemption for the year.

- A gift to a minor child of shares where the dividend income is more than £100 per tax year will be caught by HMRC's anti-avoidance rules. Although from a capital gains tax standpoint the child would own the shares, the dividends would continue to be taxed in the hands of the gifting parent.

- Inheritance tax consequences (see Chapter 23).

Capital Gains Tax Savings

Despite the above drawbacks, gifting assets to children is an extremely effective long-term capital gains tax saving strategy.

CGT can be avoided when you initially make the gift by, for example, only gifting shares which have recently been acquired and have relatively small gains. You can also make sure you gift shares in years in which your CGT exemption is available.

Income tax on dividends can be avoided simply by gifting shares that don't pay income or which have very low dividend yields!

This could result in useful tax savings for parents. For example, gains of up to £10,100 per tax year will be completely tax free, and provided the proceeds are less than £40,400 the gain will not have to be disclosed on a tax return.

Example

Jane and Steve, both higher-rate taxpayers, jointly own £30,000 of China Bucks plc shares which are showing gains of £10,000. They gift the shares to their eight-year-old son, Steve jr, and their five-year-old daughter, Abi.

There will be no CGT payable if Jane and Steve's annual CGT exemptions have not been used up in the year the gift is made. We'll also assume that these are high growth shares which do not pay dividends so Jane and Steve don't have to worry about paying any income tax.

Let's say that over the next 10 years the shares rise in value to £70,000 and are sold to pay for the children's university studies. We'll also assume the annual CGT exemption has risen in value to £15,000.

The children will be each taxed as follows:

Proceeds	*£35,000*
Less cost	*£15,000*
Gain	*£20,000*
Less CGT Exemption	*£15,000*
Taxable gain	*£5,000*
Tax @ 18%	*£900*

So the combined tax bill for Steve jr and Abi on £40,000 of profits is £1,800. What's more, the parents still have their annual exemptions free for other disposals.

Note, transferring shares to children is only worthwhile as a capital gains tax planning tool if you and your spouse have significant assets and value your own annual exemptions highly.

Where there is only one child, remember that in many cases you will be substituting two annual exemptions (your's and your spouse's) for one annual exemption (the child's).

So it is possible to transfer shares and end up paying *more* capital gains tax!

The Legal Stuff

Care needs to be taken with the legal formalities regarding capacity to enter contracts and it may simply be necessary to transfer the beneficial interest to the child.

As it is the beneficial interest that determines who will be taxed, the child would in theory suffer the CGT charge on an eventual disposal.

It would be sensible in this situation to draw up a deed of bare trust. This would state that the parent holds the legal title to the shares, but the full beneficial entitlement rests with the child.

The gift would also be a potentially exempt transfer for inheritance tax purposes (see Chapter 23). However, provided the parent survives seven years after making the gift, the value will be excluded from the estate for IHT purposes.

If the parent was to survive less than seven years, all or part of the value of the gift would be included in the parent's estate.

Note that any transfer to a child would be most tax efficient where the gift was of shares with a low inbuilt gain and you expect the shares to grow strongly in the years ahead.

The gain on transfer would then be low and, in addition, for IHT purposes, the shares' valuation would be fixed at the date of transfer, which may be substantially lower than the probate value.

It's also possible to avoid the anti-avoidance rules on dividend income if grandparents, instead of parents, gift assets. So it's possible to arrange for shares or other assets that generate high income to be transferred into the names of the children and all the income will be taxed in the children's hands.

The income would probably be covered by the children's personal allowances.

Prior to the 2006 Budget, a popular alternative to actually gifting shares to children was to transfer them to a trust of which the children were beneficiaries. There are now a number of drawbacks to doing this.

In terms of the actual transfer of cash or shares to the trust an immediate inheritance tax charge could arise when the trust is created and the trust itself could be liable to tax charges on its tenth anniversary and when assets are distributed.

In addition, if the trust is established by a parent, both the income and gains of the trust could be taxed in the parent's hands. Therefore the CGT advantages above of using a minor child to own shares may not be available if a trust is used.

Chapter 13

How to Make the Most of Your Losses

If you dispose of shares for less than their original cost, a capital loss arises. The general rule is that a capital loss can be offset against capital gains you have made in the *current* tax year.

If you still have losses left over, these can be carried forward and offset against gains made in future tax years.

The important point to note is that losses incurred in a *previous* tax year are only used to reduce your current year's chargeable gains down to £10,100, the amount of the annual capital gains tax exemption.

This is good news because it prevents the annual CGT exemption from being wasted.

Example

Justin, a higher-rate taxpayer, made the following share transactions:

- *April 6 2009 sold shares in GF plc and suffered a loss of £10,000.*
- *July 1 2009 sold shares in PT plc and made a gain of £12,000.*

The loss of £10,000 is offset against the gain of £12,000 (as these occurred in the same tax year), leaving a net gain of £2,000. The tax position would be as follows:

Gain	*£12,000*
Less: Loss	*£10,000*
Less: Annual exemption	
£10,100 but restricted to	*£2,000*
Taxable Gain	*NIL*

As no other gains occurred during the tax year, £8,100 of the annual *exemption is effectively wasted. But if the loss of £10,000 was incurred in the **previous** tax year, and carried forward to the current 2009/2010 tax year, only £1,900 of the loss would be offset:*

Gain	*£12,000*
Less: Loss	*£1,900*
Less: Annual exemption	*£10,100*
Gain	*NIL*

The remaining £8,100 of losses can be carried forward to the next tax year and potentially result in a tax saving of £1,458 (18% of £8,100).

Because losses carried forward are worth more than losses written off in the current tax year, the crucial question is, how do you ensure your losses are carried forward rather than used up in the current tax year?

Sell Loss-Making Shares

One way of maximising the benefit is to sell loss-making shares in a year when you have no other capital gains.

Example

Bill has £12,000 profit showing on Bull plc and a £12,000 loss showing on Bear plc. If he sells them in the same tax year he will pay no capital gains tax but will also waste most of his annual CGT exemption. If instead he just sells Bear plc he will make a loss of £12,000. This loss will be carried forward to the next tax year. Let's say in this next tax year he sells Bull plc. The tax calculation will be as follows:

Gain	*£12,000*
Less:	
Previous year's loss	*£1,900*
Less:	
Annual exemption	*£10,100*
Taxable Gain	*NIL*

And he still has £10,100 of losses to carry forward to future tax years!

Married Couples or Civil Partners

Another way of making the most of losses is to ensure that loss-making shares are *not* owned jointly. As we've already discussed, it often makes sense for married couples to own shares jointly so that they can make full use of two annual CGT exemptions. With losses the opposite is sometimes true. To ensure losses can be carried forward it often pays for only one spouse to own the shares.

Example

Bill and Wendy have £5,000 of profits showing on Bull plc and £5,000 of losses showing on Bear plc. They want to dispose of both holdings in the current tax year. If they sell both, the gain from Bull will be offset by the loss from Bear and no tax will be payable. However, they will also waste their annual capital gains tax exemptions. If instead Bill owns and sells Bull plc and Wendy owns and sells Bear plc, Bill will not have to pay any tax because his gain will be covered by his annual CGT exemption. Wendy's £5,000 loss will be carried forward to future tax years.

Alternatively they could sell Bear plc now and Bull plc in the new tax year, just as in the previous example. This may have the same tax consequences but may not be a desirable investment strategy.

Chapter 14

Getting Extra Mileage From Your ISAs

The humble ISA is one of the most powerful tools in the private investor's toolkit. Most couples can invest £14,400 per tax year and shelter all their income and capital gains forever more from the taxman.

However, there's more to ISAs than meets the eye. In this chapter we explain all the rules and, more importantly, show you how ISAs can be utilised to achieve extra tax savings.

Investment Limits

For the 2009/2010 tax year most people can invest up to £3,600 in a cash ISA and £7,200 in an equity ISA. You can even have both a cash and equity ISA provided your total investment doesn't exceed the £7,200 limit. The previous distinction between a 'maxi' and 'mini' ISA has been removed.

Investors must be aged 18 or over to own share ISAs (16-18 to own cash ISAs).

In the 2009 Budget the Chancellor also announced that from 6 October 2009, the ISA limit will increase to £10,200 (£5,100 for cash ISAs) for people aged 50 or over.

So provided you're aged 50 or over you will be able to deposit £10,200 into your 2009/2010 ISA, £5,100 of which can be in a cash ISA.

As from 6 April 2010, the ISA limit for all investors, irrespective of age, will be £10,200 (£5,100 for cash ISAs).

Investment Options

You can use ISAs to invest in a wide variety of different assets:

- Shares and corporate bonds issued by companies listed on recognised stock exchanges anywhere in the world.

- UK gilts and government bonds issued by other countries in the European Economic Area.

- Units in UK authorised unit trusts or open ended investment companies (OEICs), including property unit trusts.

- Shares in approved investment trusts.

Note that options and warrants cannot be held within an ISA.

Also, only quoted shares can be included. This includes Techmark shares but shares treated as unquoted for tax purposes (for example, shares listed on the Alternative Investment Market) cannot be included within an ISA, unless they are received through a qualifying employee share scheme.

You also cannot put shares you inherit into an ISA or any other existing shares that you already own. There is, however, one exception to this rule. You are allowed to invest certain shares obtained through an employee share scheme.

You would need to transfer shares emerging from a SAYE scheme or an approved Profit Share Scheme directly into the ISA within 90 days of exercising the option. This would then enable you to avoid capital gains tax altogether. The usual limits would still apply, so for a shares ISA the value of the shares at the date of transfer would need to be less than £7,200 for 2009/2010 if you're less than 50 years of age.

Losses

Just as any gains from ISA investments are not taxable, so any losses are not available for offset against other gains.

Non-residency

If you become non resident you are not allowed to continue

investing in an ISA. However, HMRC will allow you to keep your ISA investments and they will still obtain the beneficial tax treatment (eg dividends exempt from UK income tax). On your return to the UK, you can then continue to top up your ISA investments.

Using Your Spouse

Spouses are treated independently for tax purposes and therefore each spouse is entitled to invest up to £7,200 per tax year (for the current tax year). This means a married couple can shelter £14,400 every year. If you're both aged over 50 the increase in the ISA limits for 2009/2010 mean you can shelter £20,400 each year.

It rarely pays not to use up your ISA allowance as there are generally no penalties, minimum investment periods or other hidden costs.

Using Your Children

There's nothing to stop you gifting cash to your adult children so that they can have their own ISAs. All income and capital gains will be completely tax free.

Remember this could be a potentially exempt transfer for inheritance tax purposes and taxed as part of your estate if you die within seven years (see Chapter 23 on inheritance tax planning). However, the first £3,000 of donations per person per tax year are completely exempt from inheritance tax.

The Benefits of Self-Select ISAs

Self-select ISAs are ideal for active investors. They let you buy and sell shares as often as you like.

They're available from stockbrokers, including online stockbrokers and certain high street banks.

Self-select ISAs are usually more expensive than ordinary ISAs but they've become extremely competitive in recent years and there are some great deals available from some of the online brokers.

When choosing a self-select ISA, note the following:

- **The cost per trade**. These charges have fallen dramatically in recent years. For example, Halifax charges just £11.95 per trade. Some brokers charge less if you make a large number of trades. For example, Barclays charges just £6.95 per trade after you've completed 25 trades in a month.

- **Admin charge**. Some brokers such as Alliance Trusts do not levy any annual fee. Others such as Squaregain charge a flat fee of £25 per year and others such as Halifax charge a percentage, typically 5% per month (with a maximum of £8.33 per month).

- **Investment choice.** Some self-select ISAs offer a bigger range of shares and investment funds than others. For example, some offer foreign stocks, others don't.

- **Exit penalties.** If you wish to switch to a new ISA there may be an exit charge. It's advisable to check up on this *before* you open a self-select ISA. It's only after you open an account that you will discover what quality of service is provided so it is advisable to keep your options open.

- **Efficiency.** Competitive charges are only one side of the coin. You also have to have faith in the firm's ability to handle your trades quickly and efficiently.

Self-select ISAs are available from many stockbrokers and certain high street banks and other financial companies:

- Halifax - www.halifax.co.uk/sharedealing

- Barclays - www.stockbrokers.barclays.co.uk

- Killik & Co - www.killikisa.co.uk

- Hargreaves Lansdown - www.h-l.co.uk

- Squaregain (now merged with Selftrade) - www.selftrade.co.uk

- Alliance Trusts – www.alliancetrusts.com

Tax Tip

So should you use a self-select ISA? Naturally, if all you do is trade shares a self-select ISA is essential. But what if you regularly trade shares and also have long-term holdings – should you use your ISA allowance to protect your long-term investments or your short-term trades?

The answer depends critically on whether your annual trading profits currently exceed your annual CGT exemption (£10,100 if you're single, £20,200 if you're married).

If they do, then it almost certainly pays to use a self-select ISA for trading purposes and invest your long–term holdings directly in shares or unit trusts.

Why? Because if your annual trading profits exceed the CGT exemption they will definitely be taxed. By its very nature 'trading' means you are making disposals which give rise to CGT. But tax will be completely avoided on capital that is sheltered by a self-select ISA.

In contrast, if your 'paper' profits from your long-term holdings exceed the annual CGT exemption they will not be taxed until you make a disposal, with the annual capital gains tax exemption then being offset.

What if your annual trading profits do not exceed your annual CGT exemption?

If you trade through an ISA and your profits are less than £10,100 (£20,200 if married) you will not receive any immediate tax benefit because your profits are already tax free. However, if you enjoy success and your profits grow you will eventually pay CGT so an ISA is arguably still worth considering. Your long-term holdings will then be invested directly but again will not be subject to CGT until you sell, by which time they could be covered by the annual CGT allowance.

The only drawback with using a self-select ISA as a frequent trader is that you are limited to the amount of capital you can invest. If you have a substantial trading portfolio you will then end up with some of your trades done through an ISA and the others done directly. This could result in multiple orders, possibly with multiple brokers and may be more trouble than it's worth. In these cases, especially if your profits are well below the annual CGT exemption, it may be worth using an ISA to protect your long-term investments.

Equities vs Bonds

If you have a balanced portfolio with some of your money in shares and the rest in gilts and corporate bonds, it may be worth considering whether it's your bonds or your shares that are sheltered in ISAs. Because most of the return from bonds comes in the form of taxable interest, it probably makes sense to use an ISA to protect these investments rather than shares. Equity returns, on the other hand, come mainly in the form of capital growth which qualifies for the annual CGT exemption and the special 18% rate of capital gains tax.

You should arguably only use your ISA allowance to shelter equities if you expect them to generate significantly higher returns than your bonds over time.

How Should You Use Your ISA Savings?

Some investors use ISAs to save for a specific eventuality, such as paying for a child's education. This is arguably not a good idea because once you sell your ISAs the tax benefits are lost forever.

If you're saving to pay for a future expense there's a very good chance that by investing directly in equities or unit trusts, rather than using an ISA wrapper, you will pay little or no capital gains tax anyway, leaving your precious ISA allowance free to put to better uses.

Example 1

Dave and Sue inherit £20,000 and decide to invest in an equity unit trust (note, not an ISA) for 10 years. After that they intend to use most of the funds to pay for their children's education. They enjoy annual returns of 7% per year. After 10 years the fund will be worth £39,343 with a total profit of £19,343. How much tax will they pay?

It is unlikely that they would pay any tax as the gain of £19,343 would be covered by their two annual CGT exemptions.

So even though Dave and Sue invested a sizeable chunk of money and earned a respectable return, they did not pay a penny in tax on their profits. If Dave and Sue had used an ISA instead they would have derived absolutely no tax benefit.

Where ISAs really come into their own is where you hold on to them for many years and use them to generate tax-free income when you retire.

Example 2

Dave and Sue decide to invest their £28,000 in an ISA for a period of 20 years to fund their retirements. Based on the same growth assumptions as the previous example, after 20 years the investment will be worth £108,351. They now wish to retire and switch from a growth fund to an income-focused fund (ISA supermarkets, for example, allow you to invest in different funds provided by different managers and switch from one to the other). The income fund has a yield of 6%, delivering them a tax-free income of £6,501 per year.

If instead of using an ISA Dave and Sue had invested directly the outcome would be entirely different. First of all the switch from a growth fund to an income fund would result in a capital gains tax charge (in this case £9,063 assuming an annual exemption of £15,000). This means they have less capital to invest for income and so their income will be just £5,957.

However that's not the end of the story. There's still tax to pay on this income. Assuming half comes from share dividends and half comes from bond interest if they are higher rate taxpayers their after-tax income will be just £4,021.

Hence by using an ISA they end up with 62% more income than by investing directly in unit trusts.

The important lessons to learn from this example are that:

- ISAs allow you, in certain circumstances, to switch between different investment funds without paying any tax. This is very valuable if you want to rebalance your portfolio every now and again.

- ISAs are most effective when held for the long term with a view to ultimately generating income.

Chapter 15

Spread Betting:
A Fantastic Tax Shelter

More and more investors are being lured by the attractions of spread betting as a means of making money on financial markets. Spread betting offers the following benefits:

- You can bet on both rising and falling markets.
- It's easy to bet on quite exotic instruments such as foreign stock market indexes.
- You can leverage your capital by placing a big bet with only a small initial outlay.

The process has become a lot simpler in recent years and bets can now be made online or using mobile phones. The charges have also been falling as new firms have entered the market. As a result, 'spreads' – the difference between buying and selling prices – have become narrower.

Firms that offer spreadbetting include:

- E*TRADE – www.uk.etrade.com
- IG Index – www.igindex.co.uk
- Tradindex – www.tradindex.com

Spread betting is also probably the most tax-efficient way of making money on financial markets, for two major reasons:

- There is no capital gains tax on profits.
- There is no stamp duty payable.

The capital gains tax exemption is the all-important factor for most speculators. Spread betting is not a viable alternative to long-term share investment, however. Spread betters cannot ride out the ups and downs of the stock market and cannot use their betting activities to generate dividend income.

However, the tax breaks make it a serious option for frequent traders/speculators.

Example

It's the beginning of the tax year and Conrad and Rupert both have £10,000 to speculate on share price movements over a 12-month period. Conrad is a spread better, Rupert invests directly in the stock market. Let's say both are incredibly lucky and call the market correctly each time and end up with profits of £20,000 after 12 months. Because he's a spread better, Conrad will have no tax to pay. Rupert has the same pre-tax profits but will end up with a tax bill of £1,782 assuming he is a higher rate taxpayer. (We've softened the tax blow by assuming that he can make full use of his annual CGT exemption.)

Clearly this example is simplistic. It ignores charges and also assumes that Conrad has not 'geared up' his positions. In other words, if the shares rise by 20% his return is 20% and not some multiple of that. However, these factors do not detract from the all important point:

A successful spread better will end up with much more money than a successful share speculator.

It could be argued that spread betters shoulder much more risk than normal investors. The risk in spread betting comes from several quarters, in particular the time limit on bets and the potentially unlimited downside.

These risks can be controlled to some extent by the serious speculator looking for a serious alternative to buying shares or other securities directly. For example, many spread-betting firms actively encourage you to employ stop losses.

What is not so well documented is the fact that, because of their unequal tax treatment, spread betting can be *less* risky than direct share investment. Let's return to Conrad and Rupert to see why.

So far Rupert, the share investor, has been reinvesting all of his profits in new trades, even though up to 18 per cent of each month's profit belongs to the taxman. There is no risk in doing this, *provided all the trades fall within the same tax year*. Remember the capital gains tax rules let you offset gains made in one year against losses made in the same tax year.

If Rupert suddenly makes big losses he can offset these against profits from previous months' trades without any danger of having insufficient funds to settle his annual capital gains tax bill. However, when the trading straddles two *separate* tax years it's a completely different story. Rupert cannot offset losses made in one year against gains made in the *previous* tax year.

If Rupert uses all his profits from the previous tax year to buy shares at the beginning of the next tax year he is taking a big risk because he is trading with money that does not belong to him but to the taxman.

Alternatively, if he plays it safe and only reinvests his after-tax profits, his returns will be much lower than Conrad's.

Example

It's the beginning of the next tax year and both Conrad and Rupert have £30,000 in their trading accounts (the original £10,000 plus £20,000 of profits). However, there is an important difference. Rupert has a tax bill of £1,782 that has to be settled when he submits his tax return. So in reality he only has £28,218 of his own money with which to trade.

Assuming they earn the same returns as before, Conrad will end up with £90,000 and Rupert will end up with just £84,654. Rupert is falling behind because he has less capital to invest during the current year. However, that's not the end of the story. Rupert has to pay tax on these profits as well, leaving him with just £76,314 (assuming the annual exemption remains at £10,100).

In summary, both Conrad and Rupert invested in the same shares and earned identical pre-tax returns. However, because Conrad went the spread betting route he ended up with 18% more money!

When Spread Betting is Not Worthwhile

- If your annual trading profits are under £10,100 (or £20,200 in the case of married couples), the spread betting tax break is largely irrelevant as your capital gains will be completely tax free anyway. So only serious traders, or those with significant other capital gains, should consider spread betting purely for tax reasons. As can be seen throughout this book, the humble CGT allowance can throw a lot of clever tax planning ideas on their head.

- There has been some speculation in the financial press over the past couple of years that the Chancellor may be considering taxing spread betting profits although nothing concrete has ever come of this. There is also the perceived danger that an individual who is regarded as carrying out a 'trading activity' will fall into the income tax net, even if the profits arise from spread betting. There is no guidance on this issue and Revenue and Customs has not, to my knowledge, raised this argument yet. The circumstances where such an argument would be raised are likely to be exceptional and the average individual engaging in spread betting would not be at risk.

- If you're engaging in a spread betting activity via a company it is much more likely to be subject to UK corporation tax. Special provisions in the corporation tax regulations exist which can tax spread betting profits as 'CFD' gains.

- It is also worth emphasizing the potential risks of spread betting. For one, there is frequently no loss limit. With a holding of shares the most the investor can lose is the original stake. Spread betters could lose much more than this, although most spread-betting firms offer a stop loss facility.

Summary

- Spread betting profits are completely free of capital gains tax.

- Spread betting transactions are not subject to stamp duty. Ordinary share investors pay 0.5% stamp duty on all purchases.

- Spread betting is a high-risk activity but nevertheless a viable alternative to short-term share speculation.

- Spread betting is not a viable alternative for the long-term investor, especially those wanting to earn income.

- Spread betters can reinvest profits from one tax year to the next. Prudent share speculators have to make provision for capital gains tax.

Chapter 16

Unit Trusts: Another Great Tax Shelter

As we saw in Chapter 6, unit trusts, OEICs and investment trusts are generally taxed in the same way as direct share investments. Profits on any disposal are subject to tax after subtracting taper relief and the annual capital gains tax allowance.

However, authorized investment funds such as these do offer one interesting tax break: The fund does not *itself* pay tax on its capital gains. This means the manager of the fund can buy and sell shares to his heart's content without any capital gains tax being payable from year to year. It's only when *you* sell your units/shares in the fund that tax becomes payable. This means your investment can grow tax free over many years.

In contrast, if you manage your own portfolio (or employ a professional manager such as a stockbroker), capital gains tax will potentially be payable every time you make a disposal.

So if you are happy to entrust all or part of your money to a professional fund manager there is scope to make tax savings by investing via an authorized unit trust, OEIC or investment trust. The critical questions are, *who* benefits most from this tax break and *how much* tax are you likely to save?

Those investors most likely to benefit are those who are already making full use of their annual capital gains tax exemptions and their ISA allowances. This is pretty obvious – if your profits are easily covered by the annual CGT exemption or sheltered in an ISA, tax is not a worry. However, if your annual stock market profits (or other capital gains for that matter) regularly exceed the exemption, you may benefit by investing some of your money in an authorised investment fund.

The theory is that, if the fund is well managed, your investment will continue to grow as much as before but there will be no annual tax bill, leaving more left over for reinvestment.

Of course you could simply buy shares directly and never sell them. The problem here is that, unlike the fund manager, you will not be able to make the inevitable adjustments that every well-managed portfolio requires.

So how much tax are you likely to save by investing in a unit trust compared with investing directly? That depends on a number of assumptions, including how much investment capital you have, how long you are prepared to invest, your expected returns and how frequently you take profits. Almost every conceivable factor in other words! Although this issue is potentially complex it is worth taking time to investigate as, in the right circumstances, it could result in a large increase in your after-tax returns.

Let's examine a couple of examples.

Example 1

Paul and Steve are both higher rate taxpayers and both are making full use of their annual CGT exemptions. Paul invests £10,000 in an aggressively managed unit trust for 10 years and enjoys capital growth of 10% per year. To keep matters simple we'll assume there are no dividends. Steve, on the other hand, invests £10,000 directly in shares, selling at the end of each year and reinvesting in new companies.

After 10 years Paul, the unit trust investor, will own an investment worth £25,937. If he sells his units his capital gain will be £15,937 (£25,937 - £10,000). He will then pay tax at 18% on this leaving him with a total fund of £23,068 after tax.

What about Steve? He sells his shares each year and, assuming he has already fully utilised his annual exemption, pays 18% tax on his total profits. After year 10 he will be left with just £21,992.

Paul and Steve have both earned identical pre-tax returns but Paul, the unit trust investor, ends up with 5% more money.

The difference in returns can be explained by the fact that Paul has been able to reinvest 100% of his profits each year and let compound growth work its magic. Money that Steve has had to pay to the taxman, Paul has been able to reinvest to generate more profits! Steve, on the other hand, has only been able to reinvest 82% of his profits so the compound growth effect has been somewhat diminished.

Because unit trust investors can potentially reinvest the taxman's money for longer periods of time, another critical question is: "How sensitive are these results to the length of the investment period?" What we will see is that the longer you invest, the more important the unit trust tax break becomes.

Example 2

The facts are exactly the same as before except this time the investment period is 20 years. Now Paul, the unit trust investor ends up with £56,965 after accounting for tax. Steve, the share investor who pays tax every year, ends up with £48,366.

This time Paul's fund is 18% bigger than Steve's!

Paul ends up better off because he only has to pay tax at the end of the investment period when he cashes in his unit trust.

Unit Trusts vs Direct Investment

If you are an experienced and successful investor and only investing in unit trusts for *tax* reasons you could argue that you will still be better off investing directly in shares because your returns will be far higher, even if you have to pay more tax. This is certainly an important argument against using unit trusts for tax reasons.

However, as we've pointed out several times throughout this guide, it is always dangerous to base your investment decisions on tax factors alone! Nevertheless the unit trust tax break is an interesting and potentially important one for serious investors who are already making full use of their annual capital gains tax and ISA allowances.

Chapter 17

Tax Shelters: VCT and EIS Shares

A tax shelter is an investment that offers favourable tax treatment, either by allowing you to defer or avoid tax. They're often established by Governments to encourage funds to be invested in higher risk activities that wouldn't normally attract the average investor. The two best-known tax shelters for UK investors are:

- Enterprise Investment Scheme (EIS) shares.
- Venture Capital Trusts (VCTs).

Enterprise Investment Scheme (EIS) Shares

The EIS scheme offers two significant forms of tax relief: income tax relief and capital gains tax relief.

Income Tax Relief

This allows an EIS investor to obtain an income tax credit for the 2008/2009 tax year equal to 20% of the amount invested.

For investments prior to April 6 2006 the maximum investment was £200,000. However, in the 2006 and 2008 Budgets the Chancellor increased the investment limit for EIS investments to £400,000 for 2006/2007 and 2007/2008 and £500,00 for tax year 2008/2009 onwards.

This means that income tax relief at 20% can be obtained on investments of up to £500,000 provided you have a large income tax liability to utilise all the relief (as an income tax loss cannot be created).

Example

Johnny purchases qualifying EIS shares for £50,000. His income tax bill for the year is £12,000. He will obtain income tax relief equal to

£10,000 (£50,000 x 20%). He will therefore only pay £2,000 in income tax.

Capital Gains Tax Relief

Enterprise Investment Schemes offer the following capital gains tax breaks:

- Capital gains from the sale of other assets (eg other shares or property) can be held over against qualifying EIS shares purchased up to one year prior to the disposal and three years after.

- Any capital gain arising when the EIS shares are sold is not taxable provided income tax relief has been given and not withdrawn and the shares are held for a qualifying period, which is usually three years.

Example

Peter makes a gain of £75,000 after selling shares in Lucky plc, a major quoted company and is concerned about his CGT exposure.

If he was to invest £75,000 in qualifying EIS shares within three years of making the sale capital gains tax will be deferred on the £75,000 until the earliest of the following:

- *The disposal of the EIS shares (excluding a disposal to a spouse)*
- *Peter ceases to be UK resident*
- *The company ceases to be a qualifying EIS company*

In addition the taxpayer can claim a lesser amount of relief. So, in the above example, if the disposal occurred in tax year 2009/2010 Peter could have claimed deferral relief of £64,900.

This would then leave a gain of £10,100 chargeable which, if no other gains existed during the tax year, would be fully offset by the annual exemption.

These reliefs sound very attractive. The problem is that they can be very restrictive and although a full analysis of the details of the EIS scheme is outside the scope of this book, it is important to note that EIS tax breaks only apply to 'qualifying' companies which essentially means that the company must be an unquoted trading company that falls within a list of approved trades.

Shares traded on the Alternative Investment Market are regarded as unquoted for this purpose and for share investors it is likely to be only AIM shares that have the potential to qualify under the EIS scheme.

If you are interested in exploring the opportunities available under the EIS scheme, it is important to obtain professional advice.

Venture Capital Trusts (VCTs)

Venture capital trusts were introduced to encourage individuals to invest in unquoted trading companies. Normally the VCT will be a quoted fund that invests in unquoted companies. VCTs offer a variety of generous tax breaks designed to offset the risks inherent in such companies:

- Dividends are completely tax free.

- Share subscribers (in other words, those who invest in the fund when it issues new shares) can obtain income tax relief equivalent to 30% of the amount invested, up to a maximum of £200,000 after 6 April 2006. (Note that for investments in tax years 2004/2005 and 2005/2006 you could obtain an income tax credit equivalent to 40% of the amount invested.)

- There is no capital gains tax when you sell your VCT shares.

- The VCT itself does not pay tax when it sells qualifying shares. This leaves more proceeds to distribute in the form of a tax-free dividend.

On the downside, the 2004 Budget prevented capital gains tax holdover relief from applying on these investments from 6th April 2004. Therefore unlike investments in EIS shares, you can't defer existing capital gains by investing in a VCT.

Income Tax Relief

For the 2004/2005 and 2005/2006 tax years subscribers to new VCT shares were entitled to 40% income tax relief on investments of up to £200,000 per year. This relief has been reduced to 30% as from 6 April 2006.

To prevent this relief being taken away, the VCT shares must be held onto for at least five years if you buy them after 6 April 2006 (three years if you bought them between 6 April 2000 and 5 April 2006).

It's standard practice for the VCT to give investors a certificate which can be used to claim tax relief. This can be done by obtaining an adjustment to your PAYE tax coding from HMRC or by waiting until you submit your tax return.

Example

Jack earns a £200,000 bonus during the 2009/2010 tax year on which he expects to pay 40% tax amounting to £80,000.

To reduce his tax bill Jack invests the maximum £200,000 in a newly launched VCT.

He will be entitled to a tax credit equal to 30% x £200,000 = £60,000, thereby reducing tax on the bonus to £20,000.

(Note: If Jack's expected income tax liability was just £30,000, the £60,000 credit would reduce his income tax liability to zero but would not create a repayment of income tax.)

The Risks

In the above example Jack has generated a £60,000 tax saving but he ends up with £200,000 worth of venture capital trust shares which he has to hold on to for at least five years.

That may not be a bad thing: the shares might rocket in value... but they may also become almost worthless if the trust makes disastrous investment choices.

For example, if in three years' time the shares have fallen by more than 30%, Jack will be worse off than if he had just paid the full tax on his bonus.

Although the firms promoting these investments would argue to the contrary, venture capital trusts are much more risky than most other share investments... why else do you think the Government uses tax relief to encourage people to invest in them?

In the 2006 Budget they became potentially even riskier investments. The size of companies eligible as investments in both VCTs and Enterprise Investment Schemes was dramatically reduced to those with gross assets of no more than £7 million (down from £15 million).

Nevertheless the income tax credit provides a massive cushion against any price fall and, with expert advice on which VCT to invest in, Jack could end up with a very profitable and tax-efficient investment.

Capital Gains Tax Relief

If Jack's shares have risen in value he will enjoy a further benefit: the gain will be completely tax free. Venture capital trust profits are exempt from capital gains tax.

In the same vein, however, no relief is available for capital losses.

The capital gains deferral provisions no longer apply, so you can no longer roll over capital gains from selling other shares or property investments by investing in a VCT.

Revenue and Customs has detailed rules that need to be satisfied by a VCT in order for investors to qualify for the various tax breaks. It is not necessary to examine the rules here but it is important to be aware of them.

Chapter 18

Equities vs Property: Which is the Best Tax Shelter?

Your decision to invest in equities or property will probably be based mainly on non-tax factors – primarily how much you expect shares and house prices to rise in the months and years ahead.

Risk is another important consideration. Many investors used to regard shares as high risk and property as a much safer alternative, especially after the bursting of the dot com bubble in 2000 and the bear market that followed. However, the property market crash in 2008 showed investors that property investments can be just as risky as shares.

As it happens, many property investors expose themselves to even greater levels of risk than stock market investors because of the large borrowings they shoulder. Whereas shares can be bought with relatively small sums of money, very few investors can buy a property outright. As a result many investors are exposed to the perils of having insufficient rental income to cover their mortgage repayments.

As with everything, a sense of balance is important and most investors would probably be well advised to consider investing in both equities and property.

While non-tax factors are the most important, there are some very important differences between the way shares and property are taxed.

The main differences can be summarised as follows:

- **Income tax.** Share dividends are taxed at either an effective 0% or 25% (if you are a higher rate taxpayer); property rental profits are taxed at 20% or 40%.

- **Stamp duty.** Share investors pay stamp duty at a flat rate of 0.5%. Property investors can end up paying zero per cent but as much as 4%.

- **Annual CGT exemption.** By selling off small parcels of shares each year share investors can make use of their annual capital gains tax exemption much more readily than property investors.

- **Special reliefs.** Property investors benefit from a number of generous capital gains tax reliefs when they sell a property that was previously their main residence.

- **ISAs.** Income and capital gains from shares and other financial assets can be protected from the taxman by using an ISA wrapper. Certain property investments (such as property unit trusts) have also qualified for ISA inclusion since the beginning of 2006.

- **Tax deductions.** Property investors can more readily gear their investments by borrowing money and offsetting interest charges against their rental income. Although risky it is regarded by many as the key to real estate riches.

Let's examine some of these differences in more detail.

Income Tax

Rental income is generally taxed much more heavily than dividend income. As an extreme example, if you earn all your income from shares you will not pay a penny in tax, provided your gross dividends are less than £43,875. If you earned £43,875 in property rental profits you would pay £7,480 in tax.

Higher rate taxpayers only pay 25% tax on their dividends, compared with 40% on their rental profits.

Should this have any bearing on your investment decisions? In some respects, yes. For example, if you're investing for income and comparing yields on different types of assets it's worth remembering that 8% from property is no better than 6.4% from shares if you are a higher rate taxpayer. Similarly, 7% from property is the same as 5.6% from shares and 6% from property is no better than 4.8% from shares!

Stamp Duty

Property stamp duty (known as stamp duty land tax) has risen dramatically in recent years. The current rates are as follows:

Purchases not exceeding £125,000	Nil*
Purchases between £125,000 and £250,000	1%
Purchases between £250,000 and £500,000	3%
Purchases over £500,000	4%

*Note that the 0% stamp duty band has been extended to £175,000 for properties purchased before 31 December 2009.

While these rates are far higher than the 0.5% on shares, a large number of property investors will be paying no more than 1%, especially those investing in flats in regions other than the South East.

Furthermore, share portfolios are more likely to be 'churned' than property portfolios, leading to multiple stamp duty charges over time. Nevertheless it would be fair to say that, taking into account all purchase costs, including legal fees, property transaction costs are far higher than those applicable to shares and other financial assets. Over a longish period of time, as the property rises in value, these extra costs are likely to be insignificant.

Annual CGT Exemption

Such is the importance of the annual capital gains tax exemption that we've devoted a whole chapter to it (see Chapter 10). For a married couple it's worth £3,636 per year in saved tax (£10,100 x 2 x 18%). Over a ten-year period that's a tax saving of £36,360! Both property investors and share investors qualify for the exemption but, in reality, property investors get to use it very rarely, as most would find it almost impossible to sell property every year. Share investors are much better placed to exploit the exemption by making annual share disposals.

Capital Gains Tax Reliefs

If you sell a property that was previously your main residence, a portion of the capital gain is tax free. The tax-free portion is calculated as follows:

Capital gain   x   Period of occupation/Period of ownership

This is what's known as the Principal Private Residence (PPR) exemption. That's not the interesting part, however. There is an extra concession that could save you a small fortune in capital gains tax. What it says is that the last 36 months of your ownership of the property are deemed to be a period of private occupation, *irrespective of whether you actually lived in the property during that period.*

In other words, you can move out of your home, rent it out for three years, and not pay a penny in capital gains tax.

If you hold on to the property for more than three years capital gains tax will again come into play. However, if you're renting out the property you will also qualify for something called Private Letting Relief.

The calculation of this latter relief can be quite complex but, under the right circumstances, the maximum relief of £40,000 *per person* can be obtained. So if the property is owned by a couple, a total of £80,000 can be lopped off the taxable profits.

No private letting relief will be given unless the property has been your only or main residence. However, there is no need for the property to be occupied *after* the letting period to obtain this relief.

The critical point is that this quirk in the tax law could affect your decision to invest in property versus shares. Whereas most investment decisions are based on non-tax factors, this is an example where tax may be the most important factor.

Example

Stuart purchases a small residence in Essex in 2004 for £200,000. A year later he inherits another property in Docklands and decides to live in that one instead (it's much closer to his job as a fund manager in Canary Wharf). He now has two choices: hold on to the Essex property and let it out, or sell it and invest the proceeds in shares. To keep things simple we'll assume each investment grew by 15% per year and could be sold for £400,000 in 2009. We'll also ignore all transaction costs. (It doesn't really matter if you think these assumptions are unrealistic – it's the tax angle that matters most here.)

Property

If Stuart holds on to the Essex property his profit after five years is £200,000. The taxable gain will be reduced by the following reliefs:

- *PPR = £160,000 (£200,000 x 4 years/5 years)*
- *Private Letting Relief = £40,000*

Remember the PPR relief is calculated over four years: one year of occupation and three years of 'deemed occupation'. Stuart's total reliefs come to £200,000, wiping out the capital gain for tax purposes. The annual CGT exemption doesn't even come into the picture. Stuart is left with capital of £400,000 to do with as he pleases.

Shares

What if he decided to invest in shares instead? He sells the Essex property after year one for £230,000 and invests this tax-free lump sum. Four years later the share portfolio is worth £400,000. What's the likely tax bill?

Profit	£170,000
Less:	
CGT allowance	£10,100
Gain	£159,900
Tax @ 18%	£28,782

Stuart would pay no tax on the property but £28,782 if he invested in shares. The property profits are £170,000; the share investment profits are just £141,218 – remember pre-tax returns were identical!

In summary, there are very few medium-term investments that are more tax efficient than a former residence. You can hold on to it for three years and not pay a penny in capital gains tax. Further tax breaks are available if the property is let out for a further period.

Chapter 19

Non-Resident and Offshore Tax Planning

Becoming non-resident is of great interest to many people who wish to avoid UK taxes. However, it's worth noting that tax rates in most industrialised countries are *higher* than those in the UK.

Therefore if you emigrate to avoid tax, you may end up jumping out of the frying pan and into the fire!

To achieve a permanent reduction in tax it is necessary to move to a tax haven or low-tax jurisdiction such as Jersey, the Isle of Man, Cyprus, Monaco or Andorra.

In this chapter we'll conduct a broad overview of non-residence tax issues. More in-depth information is contained in the Taxcafe guides *Non-Resident and Offshore Tax Planning* and *The World's Best Tax Havens*.

In the sections that follow we'll take a look at HMRC's rules regarding residence and domicile and examine how the three most important taxes (namely, income tax, capital gains and inheritance tax) are affected by a change in your status.

Residence

There is no formal legal definition of 'residence'. HMRC's practice – based on a mixture of statute and court decisions – is to regard you as resident in the UK during a tax year if :

- You spend 183 days or more in the UK during the tax year, or
- Although here for less than 183 days, you have spent more than 90 days per year in the country over the past four years (taken as an average). You will then be classed as UK resident from the fifth year.

These rules have no statutory force and should be regarded as guidance only. For example, an individual who regularly returns to the UK for 87 days per tax year may still be regarded as UK resident. This was shown in a case in 2005 involving a pilot who satisfied the 90 day limit but was still classed as UK resident due to his ongoing connection with the UK. It is therefore sensible to accept that these requirements are not set in stone, and Commissioners decisions in 2006 as well as recent HMRC guidance have made it clear that these 'tests' are not conclusive.

For example, if you were in the UK for say 80 days per tax year, had a house here and your family lived here, HMRC may well argue that you remain UK resident. It would therefore be advisable that you actually establish your 'home' overseas and minimise UK visits if you want to argue that you are non-UK resident.

A person can also be resident in two countries at the same time. It is therefore not possible to escape UK residence by arguing that you are resident elsewhere.

It is important to note that UK residence is a question of fact and not intention. Therefore although an individual may intend to leave before the 183-day limit, if he is forced to remain in the UK as a result of exceptional circumstances he will nevertheless be regarded as UK resident.

Ordinary Residence

Even if you qualify as non-resident you may still fall into the taxman's clutches by being classified as *UK ordinary resident*.

There is also no statutory test of ordinary residence. You will be classified as a UK ordinary resident if the UK is your normal place of residence.

On leaving the country you will continue to be regarded as UK ordinary resident unless you go abroad with the intention of taking up permanent residence overseas. HMRC normally interprets 'permanent' to mean three years or more.

It's therefore possible to be non-UK resident but UK ordinary resident, for example if you go abroad for a long holiday and do not return to the UK during a particular tax year.

You will continue to be classed as UK ordinary resident until you can show that you have taken up a permanent residence elsewhere.

The consequence of being classed as a UK ordinary resident is that you will have to pay UK capital gains tax on your worldwide gains.

A person who is UK resident under the 183-day test may not necessarily be UK ordinary resident. He may then have to pay tax on overseas income to the extent that the income is brought into the UK. This is known as the 'remittance basis' of tax. As from 6 April 2008 there have been a number of changes to when the remittance basis can be used. We'll look at this shortly.

However, a person who is UK resident as a result of the 90-day test would find it difficult to argue that he or she is not also UK ordinary resident and therefore worldwide income and gains would be taxed as they arise.

One factor that is likely to be taken into account in assessing ordinary residence is whether you continue to own and occupy property in the UK.

In particular, where the use or occupation of the property is combined with other factors, such as regular visits to the UK only slightly below (or even slightly above) the 90-day average. This will be persuasive evidence that you have not taken up a permanent residence elsewhere.

However, subject to this, a person who leaves the UK will cease to be UK ordinary resident if he/she establishes non-UK residence for three consecutive tax years.

Summary

As you can see, residence issues can be fairly complex. It is useful to consolidate the above:

- Individuals who are UK resident/ordinarily resident and domiciled will be liable to UK tax on their worldwide income and gains.

- Individuals who are UK resident/ordinarily resident but non-UK domiciled will be liable to UK tax on overseas income to the extent that the income is remitted to the UK provided they make a claim for the remittance basis (or it otherwise applies).

- An individual who is UK resident, but not ordinarily resident, can also be subject to the remittance basis for overseas income.

- An individual who is non-resident and not ordinarily resident will be liable to UK income tax on UK source income and will be exempt from UK capital gains tax on all assets (whether situated in the UK or overseas) except for assets used in a UK trade.

Domicile

The concept of 'domicile' is extremely important when it comes to both inheritance tax and overseas tax planning.

Losing your UK domicile is substantially more difficult than losing your UK resident status. A person is normally domiciled in the country that he regards as his home, not the place where he happens to be temporarily living.

It is, in a sense, the country that you regard as your true 'homeland' and has frequently been described as the country in which a person intends to die.

It is therefore possible for a person to live abroad for 40 years yet still remain legally domiciled in the UK.

While it is possible to be resident in two countries at the same time, it is only possible to be domiciled in one.

There are three types of domicile:

1. Domicile of Origin

A domicile of origin is acquired when a person is born. Under normal circumstances this is the father's domicile at the date of the child's birth. If the parents are unmarried, it is the mother's domicile.

A domicile of origin continues unless the individual acquires either a domicile of dependency or a domicile of choice (see below). This new domicile will remain in force unless it is abandoned, in which case the domicile of origin is revived.

2. Domicile of Choice

In order to acquire a domicile of choice a person must voluntarily make a new territory his residence and intend to remain there for the rest of his days – unless and until something occurs to make him change his mind.

Obtaining a domicile of choice is primarily a question of intent. However, once such a domicile has been established it is relatively difficult to abandon. It would be necessary for an individual to cease to reside in the country of choice indefinitely.

3. Domicile of Dependency

This type of domicile only applies to children under the age of 16. A child's domicile of origin is replaced by a domicile of dependency if there is a change in the father's domicile (mother's domicile in the case of unmarried couples). If this happens, the parent's domicile of choice becomes the child's domicile of dependency. The child keeps this domicile unless he does not live in the territory and never intends to live there. In this case the child's domicile of origin revives.

Example

John was born in Latvia and would therefore ordinarily be regarded as being of Latvian domicile. John went to live in France and successfully established France as his domicile of choice. His son, Jack, who was born in Latvia, would also have a Latvian domicile of origin, however, he would 'inherit' his father's French domicile. This would be his domicile of dependency.

If Jack intends to permanently return to Latvia on his 18th birthday and makes preparations for this, his domicile would revert to his domicile of origin. The domicile of dependency has essentially been changed as by indicating his intention to return to Latvia, the domicile of origin 'reasserts' itself.

Income Tax

Income tax is based primarily on residence. If you are resident in the UK, you are normally liable to UK tax on your worldwide income. If you are not UK resident you are still liable to UK tax on income arising in the UK, but your non-UK income is outside the scope of UK income tax.

The terms of any double taxation agreement between the UK and your country of residence also need to be considered.

If you are UK resident but non-UK domiciled, you will only be liable to UK income tax on your overseas income if you remit the proceeds to the UK.

Therefore any dividends from an overseas company would not be taxed if they were paid into an overseas bank account.

New Remittance Tax Rules

As from 6 April 2008 anyone (usually individuals with a non UK domicile) who is entitled to use the remittance basis of tax and wants to use it usually needs to file a claim on their self assessment tax return.

If they don't make a claim for the remittance basis they will be taxed on the arising basis just like other UK residents (in other words all their worldwide income and gains will be subject to UK tax whether retained abroad or not).

If a claim for the remittance basis is made there are two key consequences:

Firstly, the non domiciliary loses the benefit of the various UK allowances. This will include the loss of the UK personal allowance for offset against income (£6,475 for 2009/2010) and crucially the annual exemption for CGT purposes (£10,100 in 2009/2010).

Therefore if the remittance basis was claimed to avoid tax on overseas income the annual CGT exemption would be lost even for offset against UK gains.

Secondly, if the non domiciliary has been UK resident for more than 7 of the previous 10 tax years they will need to pay an annual additional tax charge of £30,000 on the overseas unremitted income or gains.

There are numerous exemptions and exclusions to these provisions which are considered in detail in our book *Tax Saving Tactics for Non-Doms*.

One of the main exclusions is where overseas unremitted income or gains are less than £2,000. In this case there is no need to claim the remittance basis (it is given automatically) and there is no loss of allowances or requirement to pay the £30,000 tax charge.

Capital Gains Tax (CGT)

Capital gains tax depends on both residence and *ordinary residence*. If you cease to be resident in the UK without also ceasing to be ordinarily resident here, you will remain subject to UK capital gains tax in respect of any gains made on your worldwide assets.

If you cease to be both resident and ordinarily resident, you are outside the scope of UK capital gains tax, even on UK assets.

There are, however, tax anti-avoidance rules that state that in order for an individual to avoid capital gains tax it is usually necessary to remain non-resident for **five complete tax years**.

Any gains on assets disposed of during the period of non-residence would then escape UK capital gains tax completely.

It should be noted that this rule only applies where the individual has been UK resident for at least four of the seven tax years prior to the year of departure.

If you have not been UK resident for this period it is possible to avoid capital gains tax by becoming non-UK resident AND non-UK ordinarily resident for the tax year in which the disposal takes place.

Assuming this is not the case, and you are subject to the five-year rule, no assessment is made unless you return to the UK within the five-year period. Provided you remain non-resident for at least five complete tax years, gains realised during the first five complete tax years of non-residence are tax free.

If you become UK resident within the five tax years limit, any gains on assets sold during your absence from the UK will be assessed in the tax year you return as gains of that year.

Example

*Peter left the UK in March 2009 to live overseas permanently. He then decides to sell his shares in Kick plc during the 2009/2010 tax year. Assuming he has satisfied HMRC as to his non-residence status, he will be non-resident during this complete tax year and any disposal of his shares will be **initially** free from UK capital gains tax.*

Provided he now remains non-resident for five complete tax years, in other words until at least 6 April 2014, there will be no tax to pay.

If he returns to the UK before this date he will become liable to UK capital gains tax, as if the gain arose in the tax year of his return.

Non-UK Domiciliaries

Individuals who are not of UK domicile, even though UK resident, are subject to special rules on overseas asset sales.

Gains on disposals of overseas assets are only subject to UK capital gains tax if the proceeds are brought into the UK. This is subject to the new remittance rules from 6 April 2008 as explained above. However the rules also state that the remitted amount is to be treated as capital gain first before the underlying capital is remitted.

Example

Jack, of Jamaican domicile, has been UK resident for five years. He has recently disposed of £100,000 worth of shares in a non-UK company, showing a profit of £10,000. Jack is claiming the remittance basis.

If Jack brings all the proceeds into the UK, the full £10,000 will be taxed. Similarly if Jack remitted £50,000 into the UK, this would be treated as a remittance of the £10,000 gain and £40,000 of capital.

Inheritance Tax (IHT)

Inheritance tax is based on domicile. If a person is domiciled in the UK he is liable to UK inheritance tax on his *worldwide* assets, even though he may be both resident and ordinarily resident in another country. If a person is not domiciled here, he is generally liable to inheritance tax on his UK assets only. This is not impacted by the new remittance tax rules.

Therefore a non-UK domiciliary is still liable to UK inheritance on any UK shareholdings he may own.

In addition to the general rules regarding domicile, there are also deemed domicile rules for inheritance tax purposes. These apply to deem you to be UK domiciled for inheritance tax purposes where:

- You have been resident in the UK for 17 out of the last 20 years.
- You have lost your UK residence in the last three years.

Capital and Income Accounts

It is generally advisable for non-domiciliaries who are claiming the remittance basis to have separate bank accounts to separate their overseas income (taxable when brought into the UK) from their capital (tax free when brought into the UK). Failure to do this may result in Revenue and Customs deeming the amounts remitted to the UK to be taxable interest.

Furthermore, the proceeds of any foreign gains realized *prior* to obtaining UK residence should be kept in a separate account, along with any gifts or inherited money. Income can then be remitted from this fund free of UK tax.

Also, the proceeds of overseas gains realized whilst UK resident should be kept in a separate account. These funds will be subject to capital gains tax when remitted to the UK (but at the 18% rate of CGT).

Offshore Bonds

Offshore bonds offer opportunities for individuals expecting to be non-resident or have a lower income on the date of encashment.

By choosing an investment that benefits from 'gross roll up', no income will be taxed during the life of the bond.

It's only when encashment takes place that income tax is payable. However, by arranging to be non-resident any UK income tax will be eliminated, although clearly any overseas taxation consequences would have to be considered.

Time Apportionment

Time apportionment is a relief which investors in offshore bonds receive for the time they are not resident in the UK and is particularly beneficial for returning expatriates. As an example, if you spend half the investment period outside the UK as a non-resident, then any tax liability will be calculated depending on the proportion of time actually resident in the UK.

Therefore any expatriates who suspect that they may return to the UK, should consider owning an offshore bond for the potential tax-planning benefits available under the time apportionment rules.

Example

Percy takes out a £10,000 bond while living abroad. This increases to £20,000 over the next five years. He then moves back to the UK and decides to top the bond up by a further £80,000 (total investment £100,000). Over the next five years the fund value grows to £200,000, at which point Percy decides to cash it in. The total gain is therefore £110,000, of which £100,000 has occurred within the past five years.

Time apportionment applies because although the total ownership is 10 years, five years was spent as a non-resident and, as such, the chargeable gain is reduced to £55,000.

Summary

There are opportunities available to non-UK resident individuals to dispose of UK shareholdings free of UK capital gains tax.

Note that the position for share traders is more complex. Share traders will be subject to UK income tax on their UK source income and, as such, a non-resident individual trading in the UK would have UK income, which could be subject to UK income tax.

Share traders, may therefore be subject to UK income tax on any profits arising from their UK share dealing trade. In practice, however, this is unlikely given there would be no UK permanent establishment through which the trade was carried out.

Chapter 20

Making the Most of Gilts and Corporate Bonds

When Governments or big companies wish to borrow money they issue bonds. These 'chunks of debt' will pay you interest at a fixed rate for a number of years, typically five to 20 years. Bonds, especially government bonds, are potentially 'risk-free' investments because they guarantee to repay your initial capital at the end of the borrowing period.

Although the borrower guarantees to repay your initial capital at the end of the bond's life, bonds can be bought or sold on the open market at any time before that. The price of a bond during its lifetime is determined by the market level of interest rates. When interest rates go up bond prices fall, when interest rates go down, bond prices rise.

Hence bond returns can come in two forms: interest *and* capital growth. All bond investors earn interest but only those who invest during a period of falling interest rates enjoy capital growth.

There are several reasons investors buy bonds. Most investment experts would argue that a well-balanced growth portfolio contains a mix of equities, property, bonds and cash. Younger investors, or those with a greater appetite for risk, are usually encouraged to put most of their money into high-growth assets like equities. Older and more cautious investors are encouraged to hold a greater proportion of less risky assets like bonds.

There are several ways you can invest in bonds. You can either buy them directly through your stockbroker, just like most share investments. Or you can invest indirectly through a unit trust.

For example, high-yielding corporate bond funds became extremely popular as the level of interest rates fell during the late 1990s and investors looked for ways of boosting their returns. You can also invest in bonds via a private pension plan or ISA.

The reason we mention all this is because, depending on *why* and *how* you invest in bonds, tax can have a massive impact on the outcome. The way bonds are taxed makes them extremely attractive to some types of investor and extremely unattractive to others.

Before we explore this issue further it's essential to understand exactly how bond returns are taxed.

How Are Bonds Taxed?

The answer depends on whether you invest in UK or overseas bonds or corporate bonds and whether you invest directly or indirectly:

- **UK Government bonds (also known as 'gilts').** Interest income is fully taxed generally at either the 'basic rate' of 20% or the higher income rate of 40%. Capital gains are completely tax free.

- **UK Corporate bonds.** Interest income is fully taxed generally at either 20% or 40%. Capital gains are tax free, provided the bond satisfies various HMRC conditions.

- **Overseas bonds.** Here we're talking about non-UK bonds, such as US Treasuries. Interest income is fully taxed generally at either 20% or 40%. Capital gains are subject to capital gains tax.

- **Bond funds.** There are many unit trusts (or OEICs) that invest solely in bonds. You can invest in both UK and international bond funds and ones that focus on government or corporate bonds. If you invest directly (rather than through an ISA) interest income is fully taxed generally at either 20% or 40%. Furthermore, capital gains are subject to capital gains tax, even if the fund only invests in otherwise exempt UK Government and corporate bonds.

- **Bond ISAs and Pensions.** Many bond funds come with their own ISA 'wrappers'. In this case all income and capital gains are tax free. You can also invest in bonds through a private pension plan or SIPP. All income and capital gains are tax free.

Clearly *how* you invest (directly or via a unit trust, pension plan or ISA) and *where* you invest (in UK or overseas bonds) could have an enormous impact on how your capital gains are taxed. The investor who makes significant capital gains from UK gilts will end up much better off than the investor who earns similar capital gains from US Treasuries. The investor who makes significant capital gains from UK gilts will end up much better off than the investor who makes significant capital gains from a UK gilt unit trust.

As we keep emphasizing, tax is not the only consideration. For example, it may be that by investing through a fund you will enjoy significantly higher capital gains than you would by investing directly. (In other words, the fund manager may be a better investor than you are!) In such cases, the after-tax returns from the unit trust could still be significantly higher.

What about interest income? With the exception of ISAs and pensions, in all cases income is fully taxable – it doesn't matter if you invest in UK or overseas bonds, directly or through a unit trust.

So where does all this leave the investor trying to allocate his funds between equities and bonds?

Equities vs Bonds

Let's say you're a long-term investor accumulating capital over a number of years by reinvesting the returns from your equities and bonds. Most long-term bond investors are looking mainly for interest income because it is very difficult to guarantee long-term capital growth from bonds. There are two questions this investor needs to answer: "How much should I invest in bonds as part of my long-term investment strategy and how should I invest?"

There have been numerous studies comparing equity and bond returns over long periods of time. This research makes fascinating reading but very little of it looks at how *tax* affects overall returns. To some extent this is understandable because there is no 'one-size-fits-all' tax rate that applies to every investor. However, in many cases tax completely alters the outcome so it is essential for any investor wishing to hold bonds to look at *after-tax* returns.

Example – Bonds versus Equities, the extreme case

Mr and Mrs Edwards inherit £25,000 and decide to invest the entire amount in equities for 20 years to provide a retirement nest egg. They earn a return of 5% per year, all of which comes in the form of capital growth rather than income.

Mr and Mrs Brown also inherit £25,000 but, being more risk averse, decide to invest all their money in bonds, earning 5% interest per year. They also invest for 20 years and reinvest all their income. We'll also assume they make no capital gains or losses over this period, which is akin to investing in a new bond issue and holding it until maturity date.

Of course, it's rather unkind of us to assume that Mr and Mrs Edwards will earn the same return as the Browns. Because equities are more volatile than bonds, investors expect them to deliver a higher return – the so-called 'equity risk premium' – over the long run. However, to make useful after-tax comparisons it makes sense to assume that returns are identical.

If we ignore tax then both couples end up with identical sums of money after 20 years – £66,332 each. However, if we compare *after-tax* returns the picture is completely different. The share investors pay no tax from year to year, only when they sell up at the end of the period. Furthermore, when they eventually sell, the amount taxed will be reduced by two annual CGT exemptions. If we assume these are £15,000 each in 20 years time the result is they would pay capital gains tax on their profits of around £2,000.

The bond investors are not so lucky. They pay income tax *every* year on *all* of their interest income. Assuming they're in the top tax bracket, we find that Mr and Mrs Brown end up with just £45,153.

In other words, the share investors end up with 42% more money than the bond investors, despite earning identical pre-tax returns!

Why do the equity investors fare so much better? The obvious reason is that for Mr and Mrs Edwards their gain is reduced by the annual CGT exemption and they are only taxed at 18%. However, there is also a more subtle explanation.

Share investors only pay CGT when they *sell* an asset, not from year to year. Until this time they have full use of the taxman's money to generate further capital gains. Bond investors have to pay tax every year on their interest income and therefore have fewer funds left to reinvest each year.

For example, even if the Edwards paid tax at the same rate as the bond investors on their equity profits (ie ignoring the impact of the new 18% CGT rate and the annual exemption) they would still end up with about 10% more capital than the bond investors!

This interesting result can be put down solely to the fact that the equity investors only pay tax at the end of the period rather than from year to year.

In other words, deferring tax by investing in assets whose returns can be 'rolled up' before tax is payable can boost returns significantly.

The Inflation Danger

Mr and Mrs Brown, the bond investors in the above example, may be perfectly happy earning a lower return than Mr and Mrs Edwards, the equity investors. After all, their investment carries significantly less risk. However, by avoiding one risk they may be exposing themselves to another: inflation.

At present anyone earning interest is heavily penalised by the way the UK tax system fails to distinguish between 'nominal' and 'real' interest rates. The nominal interest rate is what the bond pays you. The real interest rate is the nominal interest rate less the rate of inflation. The real interest rate represents the actual or *real* increase in your wealth.

Say you earn 1.5% interest and the inflation rate is 1%. Your real interest rate is 0.5%. If the tax system was fair you would only have to pay tax on this portion of your returns.

Unfortunately, however, it is not! Because tax is payable on the whole 1.5%, there's a good chance that your investment will not keep up with inflation, making you a bit poorer with every year that passes.

For example, subtracting tax at 40% leaves you with an interest rate of just 0.9% which means your real return is negative.

This is the problem faced by the long-term saver trying to accumulate wealth by investing in bonds. Even if he invests in high-yielding corporate bonds, it is very unlikely that he will earn anything more than a modest real return on his money – at most about 1% per year.

For this reason, direct investment in gilts and corporate bonds is normally not a viable long-term option for anyone trying to accumulate wealth. Bonds are only attractive if you manage to earn some capital growth as well, for example by investing in an actively managed bond fund.

However, the fees (often 4% upfront and 1% per year thereafter) and tax (remember capital gains from bond funds are taxable) may absorb much of the benefit. And if you're unlucky you may even lose money if the fund manager gets it wrong.

In many ways the 'halcyon days' for bond investors are over. Long-term interest rates have fallen dramatically over the last couple of decades due to big structural changes in developed country economies that have seen inflation rates and interest rates fall dramatically. Such spectacular returns will probably not be seen again for many years.

There are only two ways to invest in bonds if you want to earn a real return on your money: using ISAs or SIPPs.

ISAs and SIPPs

If you don't want to invest all your savings in equities and want at least a portion of your assets held in less risky assets like bonds, the only way to earn an attractive after-tax return is to invest in a tax-sheltered product such as an ISA or self-invested personal pension. In this case all your interest earnings are tax free and it is likely that you will earn a return high enough to beat inflation and grow your capital steadily over time.

For example, if Mr and Mrs Brown, the bond investors in the above example, had sheltered their money in an ISA, instead of investing directly in bonds, they would have ended up with £66,332 instead of just £45,153.

In fact, it could be argued that cautious investors who want to put some of their savings into low-risk investments should use ALL of their ISA allowances to invest in bonds. After all, interest from bonds and bank accounts is heavily taxed whereas share profits are taxed more leniently, so it makes sense to use your ISA allowance in a way that gets you more 'bang for your buck'.

This would certainly be the case if you expected to earn *identical* returns from your bonds and shares. But what if, to make things more realistic, you expect your shares to do better than your bonds over time? In this case your share profits, though taxed at a lower rate, will be significantly higher resulting in a potentially higher tax bill. So you could save more tax by using your ISA allowance to invest in shares, even though they are taxed at a lower rate.

It all depends on how much better your shares perform, how long you invest and what you do with the money at the end of the day.

Chapter 21

How to Avoid Income Tax On Your Dividends

Investors can put their money into all sorts of income-generating assets, the most obvious ones being shares for dividends, property for rents, and bonds and cash for interest.

Each has benefits and drawbacks. There is no risk investing in Government bonds and very little risk investing in bank deposits. However, as shown in the previous chapter, these investments offer little or no protection against inflation.

Property rents should rise over time but your income could suffer if the property is empty for a protracted period or if you incur unexpectedly high costs associated with the property.

Share dividends also offer protection against inflation but dividends can be cut or fall away completely if the company experiences financial hardship or goes bust. This risk can, however, be reduced by investing in an income unit trust or other income-focused investment fund.

One of the prime considerations for income investors is how big the *yield* is on different types of assets. By yield we simply mean income expressed as a percentage of the amount invested. A £100 asset that pays £10 has a 10% yield. Care has to be exercised when comparing yields on different investments because of factors such as tax, hidden costs and inflation protection.

Many investors are lured by high *initial* yields. For example, a corporate bond yielding 5% appears a lot more attractive than a share paying 3%. However, some assets, in particular shares, generally offer low initial yields but the prospect of a steadily rising income to protect you against inflation. Bank deposits and bonds, with the exception of index-linked gilts, offer no such protection and you're likely to see the real value of your income erode over time.

Caution also has to be exercised when comparing income yields on different types of investment as there is often a wide divergence between *gross* income yields and *net* income yields. By 'gross' we mean income before deducting all costs and tax.

For example, if you buy a property with a rental yield of 8% there's a good chance that well over half of this will be eaten up by tax and other costs... even if you buy the property outright without using borrowed money. From the property's rental income you have to deduct maintenance costs and wear and tear, insurance and letting agent's fees and it's not uncommon for property to lie vacant for one month out of every 12.

With shares there are no hidden costs to worry about – what you see is what you get! So a dividend yield of 8% from shares is far more attractive than a rental yield of 8%.

Furthermore, dividends are taxed much more favourably than most other types of income. In 2009/2010 higher-rate taxpayers only have to pay 25% tax on their dividends, compared with 40% on their rental profits and 40% on their interest income. So even if your property and shares pay you the same income, the taxman will let you keep 15% more of your share income.

And if you're a basic-rate taxpayer you don't have to pay any tax on your dividends, whereas you have to pay 20% tax on your rental profits and interest income. A married couple, who earn no other income, can therefore each receive gross dividends of almost £44,000 without paying a penny in income tax!

Another important difference between dividends and property rents is that for higher-rate taxpayers dividends can be converted into completely tax-free income by investing through an ISA. (Basic-rate taxpayers receive no tax benefits from ISA dividends.)

The tax treatment of dividends can be extremely confusing because of terms like 'tax credit', 'net dividend' and 'gross dividend'. In reality it's quite simple when you cut through all the jargon. In this chapter we will explain in plain English how dividends are taxed. Then we'll look at some useful tax-planning strategies.

Definitions

Net Dividend

This is the most important dividend number because it is the actual payment you receive from the company whose shares you own. In other words, the cheque you receive is the net dividend. If you are a higher-rate taxpayer (see Appendix A) you will then have to pay income tax of 25% on this amount. Other taxpayers pay no further tax on their dividends.

Gross Dividend

This is calculated by 'grossing up your net dividend'. To do this you multiply the net dividend by 10/9. For example, if your net dividend is £100, the gross dividend is:

£100 x 100/90 = £111.11

This amount is then used when calculating your annual tax bill, as will be shown below.

Tax Credit

When you receive your dividend cheque (your net dividend) it will also detail an amount of 'tax credit'. This is simply 10% of your gross dividend. So if the net dividend is £100 and the gross dividend is £111.11, the dividend tax credit is:

£111.11 x 10% = £11.11

It is important to note that the tax credit cannot be used to create an income tax refund.

Are Gross Dividends and Tax Credits Important?

It's the net dividend that is the most important number for your financial planning because this is the actual income you receive. Gross dividends and tax credits are only important when it comes to doing your paperwork and filling in your tax return.

The Dividend Tax Calculation

Although the 'effective' tax rate for dividends is 25% for higher-rate taxpayers and 0% for other taxpayers, the 'formal' tax rates are 32.5% and 10% respectively. How you arrive at 25% and 0% is by deducting the tax credit when you do your tax calculation. This is best illustrated by means of some examples.

As we've said, when an individual receives a dividend, the amount received is 'grossed up' by the fraction 10/9 and this is known as the gross dividend. The gross dividend is taxed along with the taxpayer's other income.

Example 1 – Basic-rate taxpayer

John receives a £90 dividend. His tax calculation is as follows:

Gross Dividend: £90 x 10/9	*£100*
Tax @ 10%	*£10*
Tax credit: £100 x 10%	*£10*
Tax payable	*£0*

Example 2 – Higher-rate taxpayer

Jack a higher-rate taxpayer receives a dividend of £90. His tax calculation is as follows:

Gross Dividend: £90 x 10/9	*£100*
Tax @ 32.5%	*£32.50*
Tax credit: £100 x 10%	*£10*
Tax payable	*£22.5*

Jack has actually received £90. Out of this he will have to pay £22.50 to Revenue and Customs. The effective tax rate is therefore 22.5/90 = 25%.

If your dividend income pushes you into the higher-rate tax bracket, your effective tax rate on your dividend income will lie somewhere between 0% and 25%. To see why, it's first important to have a firm grasp of UK income tax rates.

UK Income Tax Rates

For the 2009/2010 tax year the following tax rates apply:

	£
• Savings rate - 10%	2,440
• Basic rate - 20%	37,400
• Higher rate – 40%	Over 37,400

The special savings rate that applies from 6 April 2008 applies only for the purposes of savings income (essentially interest). However, if you have any non savings income (eg salary, profits or rents) that exceed the £2,440 savings band the 10% savings rate would not be available. The interest would then be taxed at the 20% basic rate.

In addition, everyone enjoys a personal allowance of £6,475, which means the first £6,475 of income you receive is completely tax free. What this means is that you only pay tax at 40% when you earn more than £43,875 (£37,400 + £6,475).

It's also important to point out that dividends are the 'top slice' of income so if you earn salary or other income such as rents and interest of more than £43,875, all of your dividends will be taxed at the higher rate. Now let's see how much tax an investor pays who earns all his income from dividends.

Example 1

Phil receives dividends of £45,000 and no other income. How is his tax calculated?

	£
Gross Dividends £45,000 x 100/90	*50,000*
Less: Personal allowance	*6,475*
Taxable income	*43,525*
Tax @ 10% on first £37,400	*3,740*
Tax @ 32.5% on balance £6,125	*1,991*
Total Tax	*5,731*
Less Tax Credit (10% taxable dividend)	*4,353*
Tax payable	*1,378*

In total Phil earns £45,000 in dividends and pays tax of £1,378 – an effective tax rate of just 3%. The tax credit is reduced from £5,000 to £4,353 as part of the dividend is offset by the personal allowance. This restriction usually only applies if there is no other taxable income arising in the year.

This example illustrates that dividends are an extremely tax efficient form of income. What about a taxpayer who earns income from a variety of sources. How much tax would this person end up paying?

Example 2

Pat received the following income during the 2009/10 tax year:

- *Salary from employment with Dingbat plc - £20,000*
- *Rental profits from buy-to-let properties - £8,000*
- *Bank interest - £2,000 (gross)*
- *Net dividends from shares in Rich plc - £15,000*

Income tax of £3,000 has already been deducted from his salary. His tax bill is calculated as follows:

Salary	*£20,000*
Rental income	*£8,000*
Interest	*£2,000*
Gross Dividends	*£16,667*
Total taxable income	*£46,667*
Less: personal allowance	*£6,475*
	£40,192

Tax on Salary
£20,000 - £6,475 = £13,525 @ 20%   *£2,705*

Rental income
£8,000 @ 20%   *£1,600*

Interest
£2,000 @ 20%   *£400*

Dividends

Balance of basic rate tax band:
£37,400 – £13,525 – £8,000 – £2,000:
£13,875 @ 10%   £1,388

Remainder taxed in higher rate band:

£16,667 - £13,875:
£2,792 @ 32.5%   £907

Total tax   **£7,000**

Less:
Tax deducted on interest   £400
PAYE   £3,000
Dividend Tax Credit   £1,667

Total income tax payable   **£1,933**

In this example, Pat has received dividends totalling £15,000 and paid £628 in tax, after subtracting the dividend tax credit. The effective tax rate is just 4.2%.

Remember that dividends are treated as the final source of income when looking at which income to tax first. Therefore if you have dividends and your total income is over the basic rate band (£37,400 for the 2009/10 tax year), some or all of the dividends will be taxed at the higher rate.

Payments on Account

Most taxpayers only have to pay income tax on their dividends when they submit their annual tax return. For tax year 2009/2010 if you're filing online you need to file by January 31 following the end of the tax year (31 January 2011 for tax year 2009/2010). If you're filing a paper return you will need to submit it by 31 October 2010 (for the 2009/2010 tax year).

However, if you earn a lot of income from dividends you may have to make two 'payments on account'. These are based on your income tax liability from the previous tax year and have to be paid by 31 January *during* the tax year and by 31 July *following* the tax year.

Payments on account are not necessary if:

- Your tax liability for the previous year (net of tax deducted at source) is less than £500, or

- More than 80% of your previous year's tax liability was met by tax deducted at source.

If you have substantial dividend income, or are a share trader, these provisions may therefore apply to you.

Note that interest, which is usually subject to deduction of tax at source, would not be included in assessing whether payments on account are due.

Income-splitting Opportunities

Spreading ownership of assets between a husband and wife is one of the best ways of avoiding both income tax and capital gains tax. In this section we'll focus on the opportunities to save income tax.

The reason it's possible to split income is that spouses are treated as separate individuals for tax purposes BUT they are allowed to transfer assets between each other with no capital gains tax arising.

To benefit it's important that one of the spouses earns less income than the other. The best case scenario is where one spouse is a higher-rate taxpayer (paying 25% tax on dividend income and 40% on rental profits and interest) and the other spouse earns no income at all.

Remember that, before tax has to be paid at the full rate, each UK resident individual is entitled to:

- A personal allowance, currently £6,475.

- A savings rate of income tax, currently 10% for interest.

- A basic rate, currently 20% and 0% for dividend income.

The key is to make sure that your spouse's income tax personal allowance and lower tax rates are fully utilized. In terms of dividends, this can mean the difference between a 25% effective tax rate and a 0% rate, just by ensuring that shares are owned by the right person at the right time.

In these circumstances, gifting assets to the low-income spouse will reap enormous tax savings. In certain circumstances there will be absolutely no tax payable at all!

Take the example of a married man who is a higher-rate taxpayer and owns shares which generate dividends of £30,000. He would normally pay £7,500 in income tax. If, however, his wife has no earnings, transferring all of the shares to her would completely eliminate this tax bill.

And remember transferring assets to your spouse has absolutely no capital gains tax consequences.

However, the capital gains tax position would need to be considered when you come to *sell* the shares. If 100% ownership is transferred to your spouse (rather than, say, 50%) only one capital gains tax exemption will be available when the shares are sold.

In other words, the best split for income tax savings may not be the best split for capital gains tax savings.

However, the good news is that you can have your cake and eat it! There's nothing to stop the lower earning spouse from owning all the shares while they are used to produce dividend income and then transferring 50% (or some other suitable percentage) back to the other spouse prior to sale.

Let's have a look at an example to illustrate the potential benefits.

Example

David has a well paid job in the city and holds share investments that produce net dividend income of £30,000. David will pay income tax of £7,500 on the dividend income as he is a higher- rate taxpayer.

He decides to transfer the shares to his wife, Sue, who earns no other income.

She would be entitled to the personal allowance of £6,475 and given that the remaining income falls solely within the basic rate band, the tax credit would cover any income tax liability. She would therefore have no income tax to pay on the £30,000 dividend income. This would be a tax saving for the couple of £7,500, enough to buy a small car!

To do this, 'beneficial title' to the shares must be transferred to the other spouse which some investors may not feel comfortable about.

One option is to make use of the '50:50' rule. Where investment assets are held jointly between husband and wife HMRC automatically assumes that the ownership and hence income is split 50:50, irrespective of the actual split between the spouses. In other words, one spouse can own 99% of the shares and the other spouse can earn 1%, with income split equally for tax purposes.

(This makes Revenue's job easier as it would be difficult to identify the true beneficial interests in many cases!)

Therefore, even if one owns 1%, and the remaining spouse owns 99% of a shareholding, the income would still be split 50:50.

Where investment assets are held jointly by spouses the 50:50 rule will apply unless the couple make a joint declaration that they want the actual beneficial interests to apply (this can be made on a form 17 - available from the HMRC website).

Clearly, for our share investor who wishes to split income to save tax, without giving away significant title, the answer would be to not make such a declaration.

If 50:50 is not an aggressive enough split, and you want your spouse to be taxed on all the income, it is necessary to transfer beneficial ownership in all the shares.

Although, splitting ownership can result in greater income tax savings, it's important to point out that, if the shares are sold, capital gains tax will follow the actual beneficial interest, and not the 50:50 rule. In other words, all or most of the gains will be taxed in the one spouse's hands. This could increase the CGT payable because the couple will lose one capital gains tax exemption.

It's also worthwhile noting that the 2004 Budget withdrew the 50:50 rule for shares in close companies. Basically this will apply to unquoted and family companies where the company is controlled by the directors or fewer than five shareholders. In this case, the actual beneficial interests will be used to determine the income for each spouse.

Example

Jack is a higher-rate taxpayer and buys shares worth £100,000. He gifts his wife Emily, who earns no income, a 1% interest in the shares. Dividend income of £15,000 is received during the year.

Assuming no declaration is made by Jack and Emily, the 50:50 rule will apply.

They would each be assessed on income of £7,500, with Jack paying income tax of £1,875 and Emily paying no income tax. Jack has therefore saved himself £1,875 and only transferred 1% of the title.

It would however, be more effective for Jack to transfer all of the shares to his wife. She would then receive the dividends and there would be no income tax payable on the dividends.

However, because only one person owns the shares only one CGT annual exemption will be available when they come to sell.

What Jack and Emily want to do is to minimize both income tax and capital gains tax. To minimize capital gains tax, prior to selling, Emily should transfer sufficient shares so that Jack can make full use of his annual exemption.

For example, let's say Emily holds on to the shares for several years, at which point she decides to take her profits. Let's say the shares have increased in value to £200,000. She is therefore looking at a potential gain of £100,000.

Assuming the annual exemption has risen to £15,000, Emily could transfer shares with a gain equivalent to £15,000 to Jack. This would be equivalent to a transfer of shares with a value of £30,000 (15% of her shareholding).

The remaining 85% would be taxed as follows:

	Jack	**Emily**
Proceeds	£30,000	£170,000
Less:		
Cost	£15,000	£85,000
Annual exemption	£15,000	£15,000
Taxable Gain	NIL	£80,000

This option would ensure that:

- The ongoing dividend income is taxed at the lowest rate.
- Both annual exemptions are available when the shares are sold.

Although this is perfectly legitimate tax planning, it would be wise not to transfer the interest immediately prior to selling the shares. Although unlikely, HMRC could challenge the transfer in such a circumstance on anti-avoidance grounds. This type of tax planning will therefore work best where the transfer was a suitable period prior to a disposal, and no actions had yet been taken to dispose of the shares.

Beware of a Settlement

One of the main points to watch out for when looking at income splitting opportunities is making sure that you don't get caught by the so-called 'settlement provision's. These are anti-avoidance provisions which have an incredibly wide scope (and that's why it's important to take professional advice). If they apply they could prevent any benefit being obtained from income splitting as dividends received by the 'recipient spouse' would be taxed on the 'gifting spouse'.

One of cases where the settlement provisions could apply is where an individual gifts an asset but retains an interest in the gifted asset.

The settlement provisions do not apply to an outright gift by one spouse to another unless:

- The gift does not carry a right to the whole of the income or
- The property given is wholly or substantially a right to income.

When you transfer quoted shares to your spouse you'd want to use the exemption for interspouse transfers. This is on the basis that you transferred shares unconditionally and that the shares represented more than 'wholly or substantially' a right to income, as they also represent rights to capital over and voting rights.

The other side of the coin is that the spouse actually making the gift must also not retain an interest in the shares. This would therefore make it vitally important that the transfer was not a 'sham' arrangement and the recipient spouse actually had rights to all the income from the shares, and did not for example pay back dividends to the gifting spouse.

This is one of those areas where it's worthwhile checking with a professional, particularly given HMRC practice in this area can change rapidly.

Using Your Children to Reduce Tax

Once your spouse's personal allowance and lower and basic-rate tax bands are used up, what next? Can you transfer income to your children?

Well, the answer is yes, you can, but unfortunately a transfer of shares to children would be classed as a disposal for capital gains tax purposes, and the disposal proceeds would be deemed to be the market value of the shares. This could result in a hefty capital gains tax bill.

Just as settlement provisions can apply to transfers where a spouse retains an interest, there is also further anti-avoidance legislation that treats income from assets gifted to children as the parent's income when the income exceeds £100.

So, for example, if there is a transfer of shares from a father to his son, the income will be taxed in the son's hands only if it is less than £100 per year. If it's more than that, the whole of the dividend payment will be taxed in the father's hands. Given that he will already have paid capital gains tax on the transfer of the shares, this would be a disastrous state of affairs.

So are there any ways to circumvent these rules? Well, firstly, it only applies to *income tax* and only where the income is more than £100. So a father could transfer shares which are expected to generate significant capital gains rather than dividend income.

When the children sell the shares the profits will be subject to capital gains tax. However, the potential tax bill could be quite low because children of any age qualify for an annual capital gains tax exemption.

Note that it does not make sense to purchase shares and then transfer them to children, especially if they're showing good profits already as your profits will be subject to capital gains tax. The best bet would be to consider one of the following strategies:

- Transfer cash to your children so they can buy the shares directly.

- Immediately transfer shares after you have bought them and before any gain arises.

- Purchase the shares purely as a nominee. There would need to be a written agreement substantiating this. Tax would then be payable by the beneficial owner of the shares. As the parent would be the owner of only the legal title to the shares (ie in 'name only'), the gain would be taxed in the hands of the child.

Secondly, it's important to remember that these rules only apply to children *under 18 years of age*.

If your children are over 18 you can transfer shares to them and the income will be taxed in their hands. Of course, this isn't much use if your children are themselves higher-rate taxpayers. However, a great many parents will be in the situation where their adult children are either studying or, if in work, paying tax at the basic rate. In these circumstances there is scope to save income tax by transferring shares to them.

If your adult children are higher-rate taxpayers but have spouses who earn little or no income, tax savings could be achieved by transferring shares directly to their spouses. Of course this is not always desirable for reasons that have nothing to do with tax.

However, many young couples who earn significantly different amounts of income have very few income-producing assets which allow them to make use of the 'poorer' spouse's personal allowance and basic-rate tax band. This is one way they can.

Remember that you will have to pay capital gains tax on any profits when you make the transfer and so may want to consider following one of the strategies outlined above.

Thirdly, the anti-avoidance rules only apply to parents transferring income-producing assets to their children. They do not apply to *grandparents* (or uncles and aunts etc) who gift shares to grandchildren.

Note that any gift would need to be a *bona fide* gift. If the gift was in fact a sham and, for example, the share proceeds were passed pack to the adult who gifted them in the first place, HMRC would argue that the beneficial interest always remained with them and tax accordingly.

Therefore, transfers of shares would be useful for grandparents, in particular, who wish to transfer assets to their grandchildren and reduce their estates for inheritance tax purposes.

Example

Pete and Ethel have three grandchildren. They have a substantial estate, and amongst their various investments have £500,000 invested in an unquoted trading company listed on AIM.

This produces net dividend income of £50,000 per year. As they are both higher-rate taxpayers, the income tax charge would be £12,500.

They decide to transfer the shares to their three grandchildren. They will each receive shares worth £167,667, with annual dividend income of £16,667. As they have no other income they would pay no tax on the dividends.

Note that in this example, unquoted trading shares were used, which we have assumed would enable the shares to qualify for gift relief on the transfer to the grandchildren (see Chapter 23 on inheritance tax planning). If gift relief was not available, this may make the transfer of the shares a no go, given the potential capital gains tax liability that will arise when the shares are transferred.

However all is not lost. If the shares are in a regular quoted company Pete and Ethel could treat the transfer to the grandchildren as more of a long-term exercise and realize just enough profit to make use of their annual capital gains tax exemptions (£20,200 per year).

Using a Company to Avoid Income Tax

Using a company to invest in shares is considered in detail in Chapter 25 but primarily with respect to capital gains tax planning. However, in certain circumstances using a company could also be beneficial from an income tax perspective.

The reason using a company may be useful from an income tax position is that dividends received by a company from another UK company are completely tax free.

The extraction of cash from the share investment company would itself be taxable, and if the cash was extracted as a dividend, there would be no difference between receiving the dividend directly or from your own company.

One long-term strategy could be to use a company as a 'money box' entity. Dividends could be saved up over many years until a sizeable cash balance develops. Let's say you earn £15,000 of dividends per year. After 10 years you will have accumulated £150,000 worth of dividends with a tax saving of about £37,500.

Extraction of the funds in the UK would result in an income tax charge. However the sole shareholder could become non-UK resident and declare a large dividend. As a non-resident individual this would be likely to be 'exempt' from UK income tax with the notional tax credit completely satisfying any income tax liability.

The tax saving from using a 'moneybox' company after April 2010 could be even greater if you have other earnings pushing you above £150,000. Using a company to hold the dividends could save you paying income tax at 36.1% rather than the current 25%. Therefore the £150,000 of dividends accumulated as above could save income tax of £54,150.

Problems with Money Box Companies

The problem here would be finding a country where you want to live and that does not tax the dividends more than in the UK.

Note that whilst anti-avoidance provisions require an individual to generally be non-resident for five complete years to avoid UK capital gains tax, no such provision exists for income tax. It would therefore be theoretically possible to become non-resident for a tax year in which the dividend was declared before returning to the UK. This would usually only apply if you went abroad under a full-time contract of employment which lasted for a complete tax year.

In practice, capital gains tax considerations would be likely to dominate this type of tax planning. For example, by using a UK company the company would remain subject to UK corporation tax, whereas by owning the shares personally, UK CGT could be avoided by becoming non-resident for five complete tax years.

There's also the status of the company to consider. The company would need to either be a trading or investment company (or a combination) to gain a deduction for any costs. A passive holding of shares would certainly not qualify as a trading company and would probably not qualify as an investment company either.

Whereas this would not be relevant as regards dividend income of the company (as this would not be taxable), any future gains realized by the company would be taxed in full with no deduction for the expenses of running the company that would ordinarily be available to a trading or investment company.

The Close Investment Company provisions would also apply so any gain would be taxed in the company at a standard 28% (as these provisions do not apply just to investment companies).

Therefore, although a company could be used to mitigate tax on ongoing income, specialist advice would undoubtedly need to be taken and the CGT implications require close inspection.

Chapter 22

Future Changes

There have been numerous changes to both corporation tax rates and income tax rates over the past couple of years. This book has been updated for the most recent changes and is based on the new rates for the 2009/2010 tax year.

There are more changes to come. For example, the small company tax rate was supposed to increase to 22% for the 2009/2010 tax year. However, this has now been postponed until at least 2010/2011.

In the 2008 Pre-Budget Report the Chancellor announced some potentially significant changes to future tax rates and allowances and there were additional announcements in the 2009 Budget.

The key provisions that may affect readers will be:

- The withdrawal of the income tax personal allowance when income exceeds £100,000.

- A new 50% 'super tax' from April 2010 for anyone earning over £150,000 per year. A special dividend tax rate of 42.5% will also apply to dividends above £150,000.

In this chapter we'll look at each of these changes in more detail.

Changes to the Personal Allowance

The 2008 Pre-Budget Report and the 2009 Budget introduced a number of changes to personal allowances:

Changes from April 2009

For 2009/2010 (ie 6 April 2009 to 5 April 2010) the personal allowance has been increased to £6,475 – an increase of £440.

The basic-rate tax band has also been increased to £37,400. This now puts the higher-rate threshold (the point at which higher-rate tax becomes payable) at £43,875, an increase of £3,040 compared with the 2008/2009 tax year.

So this means that you can earn an extra £3,040 in dividends before having to pay the 25% rate of income tax.

Changes from April 2010

The big changes to the personal allowance come into effect from April 2010. There will be a new limit designed to restrict the amount of the personal allowance available. The 2009 Budget notes state that:

"...From 2010-11, where an individual's adjusted net income is above the income limit of £100,000, the amount of the allowance will be reduced by £1 for every £2 above the income limit..."

When your income exceeds the £100,000 limit the personal allowance will be reduced by £1 for every £2 over the limit (in other words, by half of the amount by which your income exceeds the limit).

This is serious blow to taxpayers with more than £100,000 income because the personal allowance currently saves you around £2,500 in tax.

Here are some examples showing how the new rules may apply. We don't know the personal allowance for 2010/2011 yet but we'll assume its £6,500 for these examples. The other rates and allowances for 2009/2010 apply.

Jack has earnings of £50,000. He will qualify for the full personal allowance of £6,500 which will reduce his taxable income to £43,500.

Bill has earnings of £110,000. His earnings exceed the £100,000 limit by £10,000. Therefore his personal allowance would be reduced by £5,000. Therefore Bill will receive a personal allowance of £1,500.

Percy has earnings of £160,000. Like Bill, his earnings exceed the £100,000 limit. However, because he has exceeded the £100,000 limit by £60,000 this would reduce his personal allowance to zero.

What is Income?

This is a key issue. What types of income does the £100,000 limit apply to – is it all income or only certain types of income?

The new rules apply to all forms of income, and will therefore include:

- Savings income
- Trading income
- Rental income
- Employment income

It won't apply to capital gains, however. So share traders will only be caught by these rules if they have substantial trading, investment or employment income.

Non-Doms

The personal allowance rules apply to non UK domiciliaries (non-doms) in the same way as for UK resident domiciliaries. However, non-doms who claim the remittance basis of tax will have lost the personal allowance in any case. So for them the income limits may be irrelevant.

The New 50% Super Tax

This was the headline grabbing change in the 2009 Budget Report. The Chancellor announced a new 50% income tax rate on anyone earning over £150,000. The rate originally announced in the 2008 Pre-Budget Report was 45% to apply from 6 April 2011 but the Chancellor increased the rate to 50% in the April 2009 Budget and brought it forward to 6 April 2010.

Whilst it's still some way below the 83% income tax rate of the 1970s, the UK has had a 40% higher rate of income tax since 1988/89, so this would be the first change to the top tax rate for over 20 years.

So from 6th April 2010 we will end up with:

- 20% tax for income in the basic-rate band.

- 40% tax for income in the higher-rate band. If you earn £100,000+ you will start losing your personal allowance.

- 50% tax for income above £150,000. Anyone with this much income will not receive any personal allowance.

Which Income?

The new 50% tax rate will apply to non-savings and savings income above £150,000.

It will not apply to capital gains which will continue to be taxed at 18%. This will result in a whopping difference between the top income tax and capital gains tax rates.

The difference could be even more significant if Entrepreneurs Relief (which can reduce the CGT rate from 18% to 10%) is factored into the calculation.

Savings income is defined in Section 18 of the Income Tax Act 2007 and includes interest, annuity receipts and gains from life insurance policies.

Non-savings income should include all other income such as employment income, trading income and rental income. Dividend income is treated separately.

So essentially all non-dividend income above £150,000 will be taxed at 50%.

Dividends

From April 2010 there will be three tax rates for dividends:

- Dividends within the basic-rate band will be taxed at 10%.

- Dividends within the higher rate band will be taxed at 32.5%.

- Dividends above £150,000 will be taxed at a new income tax rate of 42.5%.

Note that these tax rates apply to *gross dividends,* so you will be able to offset the 10% tax credit when calculating the actual income tax you have to pay.

This means that the effective income tax rates on dividends will be 0%, 25% and 36.1% respectively.

What this Means for Share Investors & Traders

Share investors will still be subject to 18% CGT on their capital gains when they sell shares or other investments. However, if they have substantial other income such as employment income, interest income or dividend income they could pay income tax at either 50% or an effective 36.1% on their income above £150,000.

Share traders will be subject to the new 50% tax charge on all of their trading income if they exceed the £150,000 threshold (when taking account of all of their taxable income). So they could be subject to 50% income tax on profits from disposals, interest and dividends.

Chapter 23

How to Avoid Inheritance Tax

It's bad enough having to pay tax on your income or gains once, but twice? That surely isn't fair! Unfortunately this is exactly what happens with inheritance tax.

In simple terms, your net assets (that's everything you own less your debts and other liabilities) are subject to inheritance tax at a rate of 40% to the extent that they exceed the 'nil rate band'. The nil rate band for the 2009/2010 tax year is £325,000.

Because your assets will have generally been purchased out of after-tax income, the assets are in effect being taxed twice.

It is this aspect of inheritance tax that offends so many people. You've worked hard and paid your taxes throughout your lifetime, yet the Government still wants to take a large chunk of your estate when you die.

In this chapter we'll look at how IHT operates and the main reliefs and opportunities available to enable you to minimise any charge, with particular reference to share investors.

Who is Affected by Inheritance Tax?

Everybody who is either UK domiciled or has UK assets, provided the estate is above the £325,000 nil rate band is potentially affected.

'Estate' is a wide term and includes any asset that the deceased was beneficially entitled to. This will therefore commonly include:

- Land and property
- Bank and building society deposits
- Shares and securities
- Debtors
- Personal chattels

Note that it is *domicile* that is important here. Your *residence* is irrelevant and you could easily be non-resident yet UK domiciled (For more information about domicile see Chapter 19). In fact, because losing your UK domicile is much more difficult than losing your UK residence, there are many people who would be subject to UK inheritance tax but not subject to UK capital gains tax!

For inheritance tax purposes you are also deemed to be UK domiciled if either:

- You are UK resident for 17 out of the last 20 years, or
- You have lost your UK domicile within the last three years.

These deemed domicile rules, especially the first one, are especially important for non-UK domiciliaries who become UK resident for a significant period (for example, if you moved here from Australia many years ago). If you're not careful, the estate will fall into the UK inheritance tax net.

A UK domiciled individual is subject to inheritance tax on the value of his or her entire worldwide estate. Therefore, where your assets are located is irrelevant for inheritance purposes. If you are UK domiciled, your entire estate will be subject to inheritance tax.

Therefore the benefit of using any offshore structures will be reduced as your estate will include offshore accounts and shares in overseas companies. However, a non-UK domiciliary is only subject to UK IHT on the value of his or her UK estate. This means that only UK assets will be classed within the definition of 'estate'.

Location of Assets

The courts have established through a number of decisions where various assets are deemed to be located. The key points are:

- Shares and securities are situated where they are registered. If they are transferable upon more than one register, they are situated where they would normally be dealt with in the ordinary course of business. If the shares are in unquoted companies, they would be located where the company in question is located.

- Government securities are situated at the place of registration.

- Bearer shares and securities used to be located where the document of title was kept. Changes in the 2005 Budget now locate the shares where the company is registered.

- Bank accounts are situated at the branch which maintains the account. However, a foreign currency account with a recognised bank in the UK is exempt from UK IHT on the death of an individual who is non-UK resident/ordinarily resident and non-UK domiciled.

There is therefore an opportunity for a non-domiciliary to avoid UK inheritance tax by using offshore accounts and holding shares in offshore companies. This is a perfectly acceptable method of arranging your tax affairs and could lead to a drastically reduced IHT charge.

Non-UK domiciliaries can also use an offshore company or trust to invest in UK shares. The taxpayer would then own shares in an overseas asset (the offshore company) as opposed to the underlying UK shares and, as such, the value of the UK shares held would be excluded from the estate. See Chapter 19 for further details on the overseas tax planning.

Each person is entitled to use the nil rate band which exempts a proportion of their estate from IHT. For the 2009/2010 tax year this amount is £325,000. The remaining estate is then taxed at 40%.

In addition the nil rate band is now 'transferable' between spouses. This means that if your husband or wife died and left all their estate to you without utilising their own nil rate band, on your death you would have your own nil rate band and theirs to offset.

However, it is not just the assets held at the date of death that need to be taken into consideration. If you have made any gifts in the seven years prior to your death, these are deducted from the nil rate band, which will result in more of your estate falling into the tax net.

Example

Jack, a UK domiciled individual, died on September 15 2009. He had shareholdings in numerous UK quoted companies, which had a market value of £125,000 at the date of his death. He also had other assets amounting to £100,000. He had no liabilities.

On 30 September 2006, he had given his grandson shares worth £110,000. The shares have done well and now have a market value of £200,000.

Jack's inheritance tax bill (ignoring any reliefs/exemptions) is calculated as follows:

Assets	*£225,000*
Nil rate band	*£325,000*
Less: utilised in 2005 gift	*£110,000*
Remaining	*£215,000*
Taxable estate	*£10,000*
Inheritance tax @ 40%	*£4,000*

Taper Relief

If you survive seven years after making a gift it will not be included in your estate for inheritance tax purposes. However, partial relief is available if you survive for at least three years.

The various rates of taper relief are as follows:

3-4 years	20%
4-5 years	40%
5-6 years	60%
6-7 years	80%

Therefore if you survive for six years and eight months after making a large gift, 80% of the value of the gift will be exempt from inheritance tax.

It's also important to point out that the first £3,000 of any asset transfers in each tax year is exempt from inheritance tax.

Example

Wilf, aged 92, gave shares in King plc to his son in May 2004 when they had a market value of £100,000. He had made gifts a couple of years previously that exceeded the nil rate band. He dies on November 8 2009.

The value of the gift for IHT purposes will be:

	£
Value at date of gift	*100,000*
Less: annual exemptions:	
2004/2005	*3,000*
2003/2004	*3,000*
Value of gift	*94,000*

The tax on the gift would normally be calculated at 40% ie £37,600. However, as the gift was made five to six years before Wilf's death, it will qualify for taper relief of £22,560 (60% x £37,600).

The total inheritance tax payable will be £15,040 (£37,600 - £22,560).

Appreciating Assets

Note that the value of shares taken into account for inheritance tax purposes is their value at the date the gift is made and NOT at the date of death.

This value is 'locked in' even if the shares double or treble. Therefore if you gifted them when they were worth 5p each, the fact that they are valued at 15p at the date of your death will not be relevant. Similarly, if you gift them when they are worth £1 each the fact that they are valued at 1p at the date of your death will also not be relevant.

Hence from an inheritance tax planning perspective it is generally better to gift shares that you regard as undervalued, for example after a severe market downturn.

This 'gift now' strategy also enables maximum use of the seven-year exemption or the taper relief rates.

Example

Debbie has shares valued at £500,000. She is considering transferring them to her daughter in March 2010. Assuming annual capital growth of 10%, and assuming she owns other assets that would use up her nil rate band, the inheritance tax charge if she holds on to her shares instead of gifting them would be as follows:

Year of Death	Value of shares £	Inheritance Tax £
March 2011	550,000	220,000
March 2012	605,000	242,000
March 2013	665,500	266,200
March 2014	732,050	292,820
March 2015	805,255	322,102
March 2016	885,781	354,312
March 2017	974,359	389,744
March 2018	1,071,794	428,718

However, if Debbie gifted the shares to her daughter in March 2010, the tax charge would be as follows:

Year of Death	Value of shares £	Inheritance Tax £
March 2011	500,000	200,000
March 2012	500,000	200,000
March 2013	500,000	160,000
March 2014	500,000	120,000
March 2015	500,000	80,000
March 2016	500,000	40,000
March 2017	500,000	0
March 2018	500,000	0

By simply acting sooner rather than later, some significant tax savings can be made and in this case Debbie can save inheritance tax of around £428,000 by immediately transferring the shares.

However, matters are not always that simple. There are a number of issues to be considered before accepting this strategy:

- The shares will then belong to the person to whom they have been gifted, and they will receive dividends and be entitled to dispose of the shares as they wish. The income tax considerations will therefore also need to be considered.

- Capital gains tax may have to be paid. The transfer of the shares to anyone except a spouse would be a chargeable event for CGT purposes. That's why it's better to transfer shares earlier, as any gain is likely to be small.

If the shares are transferred on death CGT is irrelevant, as death is not a chargeable event for CGT purposes. Therefore any gain would be wiped out and the beneficiary would inherit the shares with a cost for CGT purposes equivalent to the probate value (in other words, market value at death).

Of course, the downside is that the value of the shares then is subject to a flat rate inheritance tax charge at 40% to the extent that their value exceeds the nil rate band.

When looking at reducing your overall tax there is a trade off between capital gains tax and inheritance tax.

Thanks to the various reliefs and deductions available in many cases a gift of shares which results in capital gains tax being paid will be more tax efficient than retaining the shares and incurring an IHT charge – although, as ever, this depends on the particular circumstances.

Example

Fred owns shares with a value of £200,000. He has other assets that would use up his nil rate band, so we can assume that he faces a potential IHT charge of £80,000 on the shares if he holds on to them and passes them to his son on his death.

He acquired them for £50,000 three years previously, so the gain we're looking at is £150,000 before reliefs.

The tables below compare the capital gains tax and inheritance tax faced by Fred/his estate, dependent on whether he gifts the shares or holds on to them.

Retaining the Shares

Assuming a growth in value of 10% per annum:

Year of death	Value of shares	IHT charge @40%
1	£220,000	£88,000
2	£242,000	£96,800
3	£266,200	£106,480
4	£292,820	£117,128
5	£322,102	£128,841
6	£354,312	£141,725
7	£389,743	£155,897
8	£428,717	£171,487

Gifting the Shares

If Fred gifts the shares to his son in year one, he will suffer a capital gains tax charge of £25,182 (taking into account the £10,100 CGT exemption):

£150,000 less £10,100 x 18% tax = £25,182

The additional inheritance tax charge will depend on how long he lives:

Year of death	Value of shares	IHT charge
1	£200,000	£80,000
2	£200,000	£80,000
3	£200,000	£80,000
4	£200,000	£64,000
5	£200,000	£48,000
6	£200,000	£32,000
7	£200,000	£16,000
8	£200,000	£0

If he survives for eight years, there would then be no IHT charge. This is significantly less than holding on to the shares and passing them as a bequest – a saving of £146,305 (£171,487 inheritance tax - £25,182 *capital gains tax). Similarly, if Fred survives for five years after the date of the gift, the total tax charge would be £73,182 (£48,000 plus £25,182), still substantially less than the £128,841 tax charge if he held on to the shares.*

However, if he survives for just two years the total tax charge would be £105,182 (£25,182 plus £80,000) which is considerably more than the £96,800 payable if he simply holds on to the shares.

In this example, if the person died within two years of the date of the gift, there would have been no benefit in making the gift.

Gift with Reservation of Benefit (GROB)

We've looked at the benefits of gifting shares to reduce inheritance tax. The problem is that you may not actually want to lose the dividend income just yet. It could be tempting to gift the legal title, yet ensure that you still obtain the dividend income.

Any attempt to retain benefits associated with share ownership (such as having the dividend income transferred into your bank account) would open up the possibility of HMRC treating the gift as a GROB and including the shares in your estate when calculating your inheritance tax bill. The gift would therefore be totally ineffective as a means of reducing inheritance tax.

Any transfer of shares should be a *bona fide* transfer and not a 'sham' arrangement designed to avoid tax. You would need to ensure that the beneficial interest in the shares was also transferred. This beneficial interest would include the right to receive dividend income and the right to dispose of the shares.

IHT Reliefs and Deductions

Just as with capital gains tax, there are a number of reliefs available that can help you reduce your likely inheritance tax bill. Remember that your estate includes your liabilities so if you have a heavily leveraged/geared portfolio, the actual value of the shares included in your estate could be far lower.

In fact, borrowing money can be a useful tax-planning technique, as it can reduce the estate's value for inheritance tax purposes yet avoid the crystallisation of a capital gains tax charge when shares are gifted.

Example

Let's assume Joan has shares valued at £250,000. The value of her remaining estate exceeds the nil rate band. The shares were originally purchased for £25,000.

Her estate is therefore faced with a potential inheritance tax charge of £100,000 if she holds on to the shares, or up to £40,500 in capital gains tax if she gifts them to a relative.

One tax-efficient option would be to raise finance of £200,000 and gift this amount to her son or other relative. This would be a potentially exempt transfer and, as such, exempt from IHT after seven years (with taper relief building up after three years). The net value of her estate would be reduced by £200,000 and capital gains tax would not be payable because the gift was cash.

Annual IHT Exemption

Any transfers made during the tax year that are less than £3,000 are free of inheritance tax. If the value gifted exceeds this, any unused annual exemption from the previous year can be brought forward (for one year only).

This can therefore be a useful method of withdrawing small sums from an individual's estate over a number of years. As shareholdings are by their nature divisible, gifts of shares are particularly suited to making use of the annual IHT exemption.

Indeed anybody looking to reduce the value of their estate should be taking advantage of this tax break.

Example

Rob gave shares in Hol plc, with a market value of £10,000, to his niece on 17 May 2009. He had made no previous gifts.

He will be entitled to deduct the annual exemption for the 2009/2010 tax year and also the annual exemption for the 2008/2009 tax year, as this was unused and can be carried forward for one year. The element of gift taken into account for IHT purposes would be £4,000.

Remember that this gift would only be subject to actual inheritance tax if his estate was above the nil rate band and if he were to die before 17th May 2016.

Gifts in Consideration of Marriage or a Civil Partnership

When a marriage or civil partnership takes place parents can gift the child £5,000, grandparents can gift £2,500 and remoter relatives can gift £1,000, and these amounts will fall out of the inheritance tax net. These amounts are over and above the annual exemption.

Example

Harry, decides to transfer his shares worth £10,000 to his daughter as a wedding present. Assuming that Harry has made no previous transfers, he will be entitled to deduct the £5,000 marriage exemption and the current and previous years' annual exemptions, which will more than cover the value of the shares gifted. This gift will therefore be ignored for inheritance tax purposes.

Note that there are also additional minor reliefs such as the small gifts exemption which excludes from IHT small gifts of up to £250 per year.

Business Property Relief (BPR)

Certain shares can be passed on totally free from inheritance tax because they qualify for Business Property Relief (BPR). The relief is available provided the following conditions are met:

- The asset is 'relevant business property', and
- The asset must be owned by the person making the transfer for the last two years at least.

What is Relevant Business Property?

There are various types of property that qualify for BPR. However, as regards shares, 'relevant business property' includes:

- Shares in unquoted companies, provided the company does not deal in shares or land). These qualify for 100% relief.

- Shares in quoted companies (again the company must not deal in shares or land), provided the transferor controls the company. These qualify for 50% relief.

Note that the company must also be a trading company – shares in investment companies do not qualify for business property relief. For more information about trading and investment companies see Chapter 25.

AIM listed shares are treated as unquoted for this purpose. Therefore provided the company is a trading company and you've owned the shares for at least two years, you should be entitled to full BPR.

As regards quoted company shares, the requirement that you must control the company to qualify for BPR excludes the vast majority of investors from this relief.

If you have assets that do qualify for BPR, this will immediately change your inheritance tax planning actions, as the shares would be effectively exempt from IHT whether gifted or retained until death.

In this case, there is no tax advantage in gifting the shares 'sooner rather than later' as they would be exempt in any case. In fact, it would be better to hold on to them, as this would allow the shares to be passed on to relatives free from capital gains tax.

Chapter 24

The Tax Dangers of Being a 'Share Trader'

There is a big difference between what stock market enthusiasts mean by the terms 'share trader' and 'share investor' and what the taxman takes these words to mean.

The distinction in UK tax law between trading and investing doesn't just apply to buying and selling financial assets – it's a general concept that relates to all activities.

A share trader is taxed in a completely different manner to a share investor. The fundamental difference is that a trader will hold shares as his 'stock', much as a motor dealer holds cars or a supermarket holds cans of beans. In comparison, an investor is believed to hold shares as assets, which are used to generate income – dividend income in this case.

The most important difference between share traders and share investors is that share traders pay *income tax* whereas share investors pay *capital gains tax*.

In simple terms, share traders are taxed under the income tax legislation just like any other business, and their taxable profits would be calculated in just the same manner.

As a self-employed individual, the trader also has obligations to pay national insurance and is entitled to establish a personal pension scheme.

So which is better, being classed as a trader or an investor?

That's the million-dollar question and, as always with tax, there is no easy answer. It will depend on your personal circumstances – you have to weigh up the pros and cons and decide which tax is better for YOU.

However, it's fair to say that after the reduction in the rate of CGT to 18% from 6 April 2008 it will be rare that share trading status will bring tax benefits.

In fact, it may be that given the reduction in the rate of CGT to 18% and with the top rate of income tax rising to 50% as from April 2010, the Revenue may take a much closer interest in share investors.

As the distinction between investment and trading now becomes even more important one view could be that the Revenue will be more willing to class investors as share traders.

It's therefore important to understand the pros and cons of being classified as a trader.

First, however, it's essential to explain what factors the Revenue takes into consideration when deciding whether you are a 'trader' or an 'investor'.

Trading vs Investment

From the taxman's standpoint, an investor acquires an asset with the intention of generating *income*. For example, a share investor would buy shares to generate dividend income. Making a profit from selling the asset is supposed to be a secondary consideration. A trader, on the other hand, buys shares with the intention of selling them at a profit.

However, intention is a difficult concept for the tax authorities to get a grip on. And your own opinion of your intention will certainly not be a decisive factor! Instead the taxman uses a variety of practical pointers to decide whether you are a trader or investor. These are commonly known as the 'badges of trade'.

If you ask Revenue and Customs whether you are a share trader or a share investor, they will probably refer you to these badges of trade.

The taxman will look firstly at your motive in buying and selling and then at the transaction in question to try and obtain a full picture of your activities.

Motive of the Taxpayer

Your motive in buying and selling shares is crucial, although it is difficult to actually prove to HMRC's satisfaction. Typical practical matters that will be looked at include:

- Whether the share purchase is an isolated event.
- Whether or not buying and selling shares is your only 'occupation'.
- Whether you reinvest your profits to buy more shares.
- The amount of capital that you have invested in your sharedealing activities. For example there would be more likelihood of share trading status if you had trading capital in excess of £50,000 - £75,000.

The Actual Transaction

HMRC will also look at the circumstances of the actual transaction to identify whether any aspect of this indicates a trading motive.

In particular they will assess:

- The length of time between the purchase of the shares and the disposal of the shares.

- The frequency of the share transactions. This will be a KEY factor in practice. HMRC will be looking for evidence of a 'continuous and habitual' activity.

- Whether the shares were purchased or simply acquired by way of an inheritance or through some other channel.

- The reason for the sale. The sale of the shares to cover a financial 'emergency' may make the likelihood of the transaction being classed as trading less likely.

- Are you claiming a tax loss? Trying to persuade HMRC that you are a trader when you have incurred a sizeable loss on share dealing activities would be much more difficult than if there were taxable profits.

- Whether any finance was obtained for the share purchases or to fund the share trading activity, for example office costs and computer equipment. A large loan to purchase shares may mean that the interest payments would offset the dividend payments. In such a case there would be good grounds for arguing that the sole opportunity to make a profit would be to dispose of the shares. This would then increase the likelihood of a trading motive.

- Dividend policy of the company in question. If the company has historically paid no dividends, this would strengthen your argument for trading status, as you would be looking to dispose of the shares to realise a profit.

- Type of shares/securities purchased. Shares that pay no income might be more easily viewed as trading than investment assets.

- Do your share dealing activities resemble a trading operation?

That last point is crucial and in a sense sums up all the other factors. Does the taxpayer give the appearance of carrying on a trade? Or as one judge put it, what we're looking for is a *"deliberate and organised scheme of profit making"*.

The buying and selling frequency, amount of capital invested, method of financing and so on all point to whether you are engaged in a 'scheme of profit making', and it is these factors in which Revenue and Customs is most interested.

Unfortunately it's not possible to simply write a list of actions you should take which will guarantee trading or investment status. If you believe your actions make you a share trader or investor, you would need to complete your tax return on that basis, with your share profits being regarded as trading income or capital gains according to your view.

I would suggest that you make clear what you are doing in a letter accompanying your tax return, allowing Revenue and Customs the opportunity to review your position if required.

You would have to build a 'pack' of evidence to support your status, considering as many of the above factors as possible.

As we shall see, however, share trading status will not now be of benefit to most share speculators.

Financial Assets vs Other Assets

There has historically been a general presumption that the purchase of income-producing assets would *usually* be classed as investing.

From the taxman's standpoint, shares have been more likely to be held as investments. In particular, one judge has said:

"... Where the question is whether an individual engaged in speculative dealings in securities is carrying on a trade, the prima facie presumption would be ... that he is not."

Clearly if there are other 'badges of trade' that apply, the presumption against trading could be reversed. Although there is a presumption against trading, this is not the end of the matter.

If you have a job in the financial markets this does not automatically mean your private share dealings will be classed as trading. Again, it will depend on the application of the general principles to assess whether you are actually in business on your own account and purchasing shares with the intention of resale at a profit.

Having said this, being employed in an associated industry would certainly be another factor to take into account and when combined with other relevant factors would strengthen a trading argument.

Whether the reduction in the rates of CGT will mean the Revenue will be more likely to argue for trading status in suitable cases awaits to be seen.

Summary

There is no single test you have to pass to be treated as a share trader. Instead your overall circumstances will be examined.

The main 'badges of trade' that will be looked at are:

- Frequency of buying and selling.
- The amount of capital at stake.
- How you came to own the shares. (Did you buy them yourself or were they received as a gift?)
- Type of shares purchased, for example, ones that generate no income.
- Method of finance.
- Whether you are claiming trading loss relief.
- Whether your activities resemble a trading operation.

So why would you want to be classed as an investor rather than a trader, or vice-versa? In the sections that follow we list most of the benefits and drawbacks of share trader status, followed by some detailed numerical comparisons.

Share Trading - Advantages

Advantage #1
Expenses

One of the main advantages of being taxed as a share trader is that a claim can be made to offset any expenses incurred 'wholly and exclusively' for the purposes of the share trading activity.

This is a potentially wide provision and could allow a whole variety of additional expenses to be claimed – provided they each satisfy the 'wholly and exclusively' requirement.

Remember that for a share *investor*, the costs that can be deducted when calculating capital gains tax are restricted to the actual purchase cost of the shares and the other incidental expenses of buying and selling (usually just stamp duty and broker's fees).

This therefore gives a share trader an advantage over a share investor.

Types of expenses that could be claimed include:

- Office rent
- Utility bills and council tax
- Interest on a loan for the purposes of the trade. This could include a loan used to buy shares or the funds could be used to purchase equipment that would be used in the trade (for example, office equipment and computers).
- Capital allowances (discussed below).
- Professional subscriptions.
- Research materials, including books and share magazines.
- Share dealing expenses such as stockbroker fees.
- Stamp duty.
- Employee salaries.
- Online share services, eg access to premium share bulletin boards.

For a serious share dealer the opportunity to offset these additional expenses against the trading income could be worth a considerable sum.

This is particularly the case where you deal in shares as a serious and organised activity on a frequent basis, in other words if you are a full-time professional trader. It's this type of person who is any case more likely to be classed as a share trader.

Example

Steven disposes of shares worth £300,000 during the 2009/2010 tax year. The cost of these shares including dealing fees and stamp duty was £175,000. Steven is therefore looking at a profit of £125,000.

If Steven has no other employment and share trading is his full time activity he may incur the following expenses:

- *Subscription to share trading website*   *£2,080*
- *Office rent*   *£25,000*
- *Investment analysis*   *£17,000*
- *Council tax*   *£2,500*
- *Utility bills*   *£1,500*
- *Share trading books*   *£750*
- *Share charting software*   *£2,000*

He would be able to claim a deduction for these expenses when calculating his taxable profits. Deducting these expenses would leave a trading profit of £74,170. If he is a 40% taxpayer, his tax bill would be £29,668.

Advantage #2
Capital Allowances

When you buy an asset that is used in your trade, the business is given capital allowances, which allow a percentage of the cost to be 'released' each year and treated as a tax-deductible expense.

There are many different capital allowances, depending on the nature of the asset. The most important one for share traders would be the 'plant and machinery' allowance.

The assets most likely to qualify for plant and machinery allowances in this case would be computers and office equipment. The rate of tax relief is 20% per year as from 6th April 2008.

Example

An item of plant purchased for £10,000 would qualify for capital allowances as follows:

Year 1 (20% x £10,000)	*£2,000*
Year 2 (20% x (£10,000 - £2,000))	*£1,600*
Year 3 (20% x (£10,000 - £3,600))	*£1,280*
...and so on.	

Most important, however, there is also a new annual investment allowance that provides for a 100% capital allowance on qualifying expenditure of up to £50,000.

Therefore a trader who spends money on a new computer system may be entitled to a 100% deduction of the cost in the period the computer was purchased. A share investor purchasing the identical computer system would not be eligible for any tax relief.

Any expenditure in excess of £50,000 could also qualify for the special 40% 'first year allowance' announced in the 2009 Budget.

Advantage #3
Pension Contributions

Profits from a share dealing trade are classed as 'earnings' for the purpose of making pension fund contributions, which qualify for attractive tax relief.

The pension regime changed dramatically on April 6th 2006 (also known as A-Day). Pensions are now much more attractive than they were before with bigger contribution limits and much more flexibility.

In particular, you'll be able to contribute 100% of your earnings subject to a maximum contribution of £245,000 in the 2009/2010 tax year.

Note that there is a minimum level of £3,600 that most individuals can invest. This is irrespective of the actual level of income during the year. This means that almost all share investors will qualify for some tax relief on pension contributions.

All allowable contributions attract 20% tax relief at source. So, for a gross contribution of £10,000, a sum of £8,000 is paid by you to the pension provider. The pension provider credits the extra £2,000 to the plan and subsequently claims this back from the taxman.

Higher rate taxpayers can claim the extra 20% when they submit their tax returns.

In the 2009 Budget it was announced that, as from 6 April 2011, tax relief for individuals with an annual income of £150,000 or more will be restricted. Relief for pension contributions will be gradually withdrawn and those earning over £180,000 will only enjoy basic-rate tax relief.

Revenue & Customs has also published some nasty penalties to stop high earners maxing out their pension contributions this year and next year.

These "anti-forestalling" provisions may apply if you have earned £150,000 or more in any tax year from 2007/8 onwards.

The good news is you can still enjoy higher-rate tax relief for the next two years even if your income is or was £150,000 or more, providing you continue as normal with your 'existing regular' pension contributions. For example, if you've been contributing £2,000 per month over the last couple of years, you can carry on doing so until April 2011 and enjoy the maximum tax relief.

By 'regular' HMRC generally means monthly or quarterly contributions – anything less frequent, such as lump sum annual contributions, will be caught by the anti-forestalling provisions.

Having said that, you will not generally be penalised if your total annual contributions are no more than £20,000.

In summary, there is still scope for those earning £150,000 or more to enjoy higher-rate tax relief for the next couple of years, providing you fully understand the anti-forestalling provisions. Those affected should read the following document:

www.hmrc.gov.uk/budget2009/pensions-individuals-1550.pdf

Advantage #4
Trading Losses

Capital losses are examined in Chapter 13. Broadly speaking, they are either offset against current year gains or carried forward to offset against future capital gains. Losses incurred in a trade are much more flexible. They can be:

- Offset against other income earned during the tax year.
- Carried forward against future profits arising from the same trade.
- Carried back against income earned in the previous tax year.
- Offset against capital gains in certain circumstances.

In summary, trading losses can be offset against other sources of income such as your salary (capital losses cannot) and can generate a tax refund (excess capital losses can only be carried forward for use in future tax years).

Example 1

Patrick deals in shares. He is a 40% taxpayer. His tax position for tax years 2006/2007 to 2009/2010 is as follows:

	Taxable profit	**Tax paid**
2006/2007	*£30,000*	*£12,000*
2007/2008	*£45,000*	*£18,000*
2008/2009	*-£20,000*	*NIL*
2009/2010	*£5,000*	*£2,000*

The loss incurred in 2008/2009 could be carried back to 2007/2008. This would therefore give rise to a repayment of income tax of £8,000. By contrast if Patrick was classed as a share investor, the loss would be carried forward to 2009/2010 and then only £5,000 would be offset.

Example 2

Jack is employed as a City broker. In the 2009/2010 tax year he earns a salary of £60,000. Tax deducted is approximately £15,400. Jack is a keen share trader and spends all his spare time playing the stock market. Unfortunately for Jack, his shares have taken a hammering, and he realizes a loss of £30,000. This loss will be offset against his employment income for the period and his revised tax charge will be:

Income	*£60,000*
Less: Loss	*£30,000*
Less: Personal allowance	*£6,475*
Income	*£23,525*
£23,525 @ 20%	*£4,705*

He has already paid £15,400 in tax so he is entitled to a refund of around £10,695.

Provisions in the 2009 Budget now provide for a temporary 3 year carry back for traders. This means that trading losses of up to £50,000 incurred in tax years 2008/2009 or 2009/2010 can be carried back to tax years 2006/2007 and set off against profits previously taxed.

However, in many cases traders may be caught by special anti avoidance rules aimed at restricting loss relief. These provisions state that where a trade is carried on in a 'non active' capacity the amount of loss relief that can be claimed against other income will be restricted to a maximum of £25,000. In addition, if the loss also arose from a tax avoidance arrangement no loss relief will be given.

A 'non active' trade is defined as one where you spend on average less than 10 hours per week in the trading activities.

Therefore if you were share trading 'on the side' in addition to another job you would need to ensure that you exceeded the 10 hours per week requirement to obtain relief for losses in excess of £25,000.

Advantage #5
Personal Allowance

If you have earned no other income during the tax year, you will be entitled to offset your personal allowance (£6,475 for the 2009/2010 tax year) against your trading profits.

If all your income comes from capital gains you would not be entitled to offset the personal allowance.

Advantage #6
Share Identification Rules

The share matching rules (see Chapter 4) only apply for capital gains tax purposes. This could give a share trader an added advantage over a share investor.

Remember that the matching rules for individuals match share sales with shares bought on:

- The same day
- The next 30 days
- The 'new 1985 pool'

These rules do not apply to traders. Instead the normal rules regarding calculation of profits and losses would come into force.

Under normal accountancy principles, a share trader would therefore match shares on the basis of 'Last In First Out' (LIFO).

Example

Pat buys shares as follows:

- *31/05/2001*   *5,000 at £1.90 each*
- *17/06/2004*   *3,000 at £1.75 each*
- *19/08/2005*   *5,000 at £2.10 each*
- *25/06/2009*   *5,000 at £1.95 each*

He sells 5,000 shares on June 20 2009 for £2.20 each.

If the capital gains tax rules applied, Pat's disposal would be matched with the acquisition on 25 June 2009. The cost of the shares for tax purposes would be £1.95 each, resulting in a taxable profit of 25p per share. The taxable gain would therefore be £1,250 (5,000 x 25p).

However, if he is classed as a share trader, the disposal would be matched with the 2005 acquisition and the gain arising would be just £500.

Share Trading - Disadvantages

"Great," you might be thinking, "How do I persuade HMRC that I'm a share trader?" Although the advantages above do seem quite impressive, this is not the whole story. As with most important tax decisions, there are benefits and drawbacks to take into account.

The disadvantages are just as persuasive as the advantages. Again, it all depends on your particular circumstances.

Let's have a look at some of the disadvantages of being classified as a share trader:

Disadvantage #1
Rates of Tax

After 5 April 2008 this is perhaps the single biggest drawback to share trader status and is the reason why most share investors will want to retain their share investor status.

The rate of capital gains tax on disposals after 5 April 2008 is now a single rate of 18% irrespective of the level of your gains or other income (before this date the rate of CGT was based on your marginal rate of income tax and therefore could be up to 40%).

This means that when they sell shares or other financial assets, share investors will be taxed at 18% on the gain that is made.

Any income from the investments such as dividends or interest, will still be subject to the standard rates of income tax. These rates of income tax are currently up to 25% for dividends and 40% on interest.

What about share traders?

Well any profit that they make when they sell shares is classed as income – not capital gains (which is why the income tax loss relief rules mentioned above apply). Therefore they'll still be subject to the standard rates of income tax on all their income from their share trading activities. This means their stock market profits and any trading income will be taxed at rates of up to 40% in 2009/2010. As from 2010 if they earn over £150,000 they will face a 50% income tax rate.

This is a huge difference and in most cases will mean that share traders will be at a huge tax disadvantage to share investors.

It would only really be if a share trader was paying tax at the basic rate of tax that the reduced CGT rate may not be a big issue.

Share traders with income within the basic rate tax band (in other words income less than £43,875) will only pay income tax at 20%, rather than 40%. In this case the 18% CGT rate is not significantly different.

In practice most individuals who are classed as share traders are likely to be higher-rate taxpayers (at least for some tax years).

Disadvantage #2
National Insurance

As your profits are treated as trading income, they are subject to national insurance, just as the profits from any other sole trader business. By contrast gains from share investments are not subject to national insurance.

A self employed share trader would be required to pay the following national insurance contributions:

- **Class 2** contributions – these are fixed at £2.40 per week for the 2009/2010 tax year. Annual bill: £124.80

- **Class 4** contributions – 8% on profits between the lower and upper profit limits and 1% on profits above the upper profit limit.

For tax year 2009/2010, the lower earning limit is £5,715 and the upper earning limit is £43,875. The Class 2 contributions are not very onerous but the Class 4 contributions essentially amount to an extra 8% to 9% tax charge, resulting in an overall tax rate of almost 50% for higher-rate taxpayers.

Example

John makes profits of £60,000 per year from his share trading activities. His national insurance is calculated as follows:

£43,875 - £5,715 @ 8%	*£3,052.8*
£60,000 - £43,875 @ 1%	*£161.25*
Class 4 national insurance	*£3,214.05*
Class 2 national insurance	*£124.8*

Total national insurance	***£3,338.85***

Table 4 shows the total national insurance bill for different levels of profit during the 2009/2010 tax year. You'll see how the national insurance bill increases quite rapidly up to profits of £50,000, then the increases level off as the 8% rate is replaced by the additional 1% rate.

TABLE 4: SHARE TRADER – NAT. INSURANCE

Profits £	National Insurance £
10,000	468
20,000	1,268
30,000	2,068
40,000	2,868
50,000	3,239
60,000	3,339
70,000	3,439
80,000	3,539
90,000	3,639
100,000	3,739
130,000	4,039
150,000	4,239
180,000	4,539
200,000	4,739

Whether this national insurance bill is worth paying depends on whether the benefits of share trader status, outlined above, more than cover this cost. We'll look at some overall calculations later.

Disadvantage #2
Loss of Capital Gains Tax Reliefs

This is one of the most important factors weighing against share trader treatment.

For small investors the loss of the annual CGT exemption would probably prove disastrous from a tax-planning angle.

Small investors are unlikely to obtain trader treatment in the first instance. However, even the more wealthy trader could suffer from losing capital gains tax reliefs, in particular the annual exemption.

Unlike capital gains tax, income tax offers only one 'automatic' relief: the personal allowance. This allowance is far smaller than the annual capital gains tax exemption and would already be fully utilized if the share trader had other income.

As a rule of thumb, if you are subject to the basic-rate of income tax and the expenses you can now claim as a share trader do not exceed your annual capital gains tax exemption you will be no better off than when you were classified as an investor.

In fact, your expenses would have to more than exceed the capital gains tax exemption to also take account of your new national insurance bill and the slightly higher tax rate.

The annual CGT exemption is £10,100 in the case of one individual but £20,200 in the case of a married couple who own shares jointly. So the share trader would have to incur tax-deductible expenditure of more than £10,100 or maybe £20,200 before any tax savings are made from share trader status... and that doesn't even take national insurance into account and assumes that the share trader is paying tax at 20%.

If the share trader was a 40% taxpayer the deductible expenses would have to be massive to offset the additional 22% tax payable and the loss of the annual CGT exemption. This is made even worse after April 2010 if the share trader is subject to the new 50% rate of income tax. In this case there would be an additional 32% tax payable by the share trader (and that's ignoring the NIC charge).

If the individual has no other sources of income then the benefit of the personal allowance must also be brought into the calculation. In this case, your tax-deductible expenses must only exceed £3,625 (£10,100 - £6,475) before any benefit is gained. Once again this ignores national insurance and the fact that the basic rate is 2% above the CGT rate.

So share trader status has its benefits (mainly tax-deductible expenses) but also drawbacks (mainly the increased tax rates, loss of CGT reliefs and national insurance).

Disadvantage #3
Tax Payments

Share traders, just like other sole traders, have to make income tax payments *during* the tax year and shortly after the end of the tax year.

With share investors it's completely different. Capital gains tax is only payable by January 31 of the *following* tax year. This gives share investors a valuable cash flow advantage as they can hold on to the taxman's money for up to 12 months longer.

Disadvantage #4
Residency Issues

If you're planning to move overseas and become non-resident, being classed as a UK share trader could be disastrous. An individual who becomes non-resident and non-UK ordinarily resident is exempt from UK capital gains tax on UK or overseas assets. This means that a share investor could become non-resident/ordinarily resident and sell UK shares with no UK taxes to pay. If the investor chooses an overseas country that doesn't have capital gains tax, tax will be avoided altogether.

By contrast individuals who trade in the UK are still in principle taxed on their profits even if they are non-resident. In many cases this is only so if there is a UK permanent establishment. UK investment managers and brokers can in certain circumstances constitute a 'permanent establishment' in the UK though.

They could also be taxed in the overseas jurisdiction as well (although relief would be available to prevent a double tax charge). So a non-resident share investor can enjoy advantages a non-resident share trader can not.

Trading vs Investment: Numerical Examples

So how much do you stand to gain or lose by being classed as a share trader? Table 5 shows the total tax payable by traders and investors at different profit levels. There are two columns for investors (one for a single investor, the other for a married couple) and two columns for traders (one for a sole trader, the other for a married couple in partnership).

These tables are based on the taxpayers having no other taxable income. It's also important to note that the table assumes that the traders have no deductible expenditure (we incorporate that in the next example).

TABLE 5: TRADING VS INVESTMENT
Total Tax Bills Compared
(Assuming no tax-deductible expenditure)

Profits £	1 Investor £	2 Investors £	Sole Trader £	Partnership £
10,000	0	0	1,173	250
20,000	1,782	0	3,973	2,345
30,000	3,582	1,764	6,773	5,145
40,000	5,382	3,564	8,798	7,945
50,000	7,182	5,364	13,169	10,745
60,000	8,982	7,164	17,269	13,545
70,000	10,782	8,964	21,369	16,345
80,000	12,582	10,764	25,469	17,596
90,000	14,382	12,564	29,569	22,238
100,000	16,182	14,364	33,669	26,338
110,000	17,982	16,164	37,769	30,438
120,000	19,782	17,964	41,869	34,538
130,000	21,582	19,764	45,969	38,638
140,000	23,382	21,564	50,069	42,738
150,000	25,182	23,364	54,169	46,838

The message from the table is clear: there is no tax benefit to be derived from share trader status. The share investor comes out on top thanks to the flat 18% rate of CGT, the annual CGT exemption and the fact that no national insurance is payable.

But what if there are significant costs, such as software, rent and subscriptions? Does this make trader classification more appealing?

An individual earning profits of £100,000 would pay capital gains tax of £16,182 or income tax and national insurance of £33,669. Therefore, in order to make share trader treatment worthwhile from a tax perspective, tax savings of over £17,487 would need to be achieved, which would require an exorbitant level of tax deductible costs.

Let's take an unrealistic example and assume a share trader makes £100,000 buying and selling shares but incurs expenses of £40,000. How would this impact on the final tax bill?

His tax as a sole trader would be:

	£
Profits (£100,000 - £40,000)	60,000
Personal allowance	-6,475
Taxable income	53,525

Income tax:

£37,400 @ 20%	7,480
£16,125 @ 40%	6,450
Total income tax	13,930
National insurance	3,339

Total income tax and national insurance £17,269

Even if the trader can deduct costs of up to £40,000 that the investor cannot, share trading status is still not attractive. The trader still pays total tax of £17,269 compared with the investor's £16,182.

In summary:

- For most people it will always be beneficial to be classed as a share investor. The reduction in the rate of CGT for investors and ability to offset one or maybe two annual CGT exemptions means that you would have to have a huge and unrealistic amount of tax deductible expenditure before you could even consider share trader status being more attractive than investor status.

- It would only be if there were also other aspects of share trader treatment that are important to you, such as the ability to offset losses or make pension contributions, that you should even consider it.

Remember there is no box to tick on your tax return to obtain share trader treatment — it's up to you to self assess your tax liability and complete your return on the basis of trading treatment if you feel this applies.

However, there are carefully defined rules as to when an individual will be regarded as trading as opposed to investing.

Chapter 25

Setting Up a Company to Save Tax

Serious share traders and investors often ask whether they should set up a company and whether this will produce attractive tax savings. In this chapter we'll take a detailed look at all the pros and cons.

Even after changes to company tax announced in the 2005, 2006 and 2007 Budgets, including the scrapping of the 0% tax rate on the first £10,000 of company profits and the increase in the rate of corporation tax to (currently) 21%, many ordinary businesses are still far better off incorporating.

In recent years using a company has also been a popular tax-avoidance route for property investors. The idea is that, because corporation tax rates are generally very low, a company investor will earn far higher after-tax returns, which can be used to invest in new properties.

In this chapter we'll examine whether share investors and traders can follow a similar route. One of the main obstacles for share *investors* is the so-called Close Investment Company (CIC) provisions – these could make using a share *investment* company a costly alternative to direct ownership. Share *traders*, on the other hand, could potentially enjoy tax savings by setting up a company.

Offshore tax planning is also increasingly of interest to those with significant income and assets. Those wanting to escape the UK taxman often ask whether they can set up an offshore company located in a tax haven. It's possible but difficult – again we'll look at how and in what circumstances this could be achieved.

How Would a Company Work?

If you deal in shares as an individual, the profits are fully taxed in your hands, even if they are reinvested. Company profits are also fully taxed. However, there is no personal tax to pay by the company owner unless cash is actually extracted from the company, either as a salary or a dividend. The advantage is that although tax is payable on the company profits, corporation tax rates are much lower than the higher rate of income tax, leaving the company with more funds to reinvest.

How the company is taxed will be influenced by whether the buying and selling amounts to share trading or share investing. This is the crucial factor.

Corporation Tax Rates

Company tax rates are generally much lower than income tax rates. Current corporation tax rates can be simply summarised as follows:

Tax Payable By Companies

On profits between £0 and £300,000	21%
On profits between £300,000 and £1.5m	29.75%
On profits over £1.5m	28%

So, for example, a company with profits of £40,000 will pay corporation tax at 21%. The total corporation tax bill will be £8,400.

If your profits are £350,000 you will pay 21% tax on the first £300,000 and 29.75% on the extra £50,000.

Once profits exceed £1.5 million the calculation is simple – all profits are taxed at a single rate of 28%.

Note that, starting with the 2010/2011 tax year, the small company tax rate may increase to 22%.

Why Use a Company?

Many businesses (both trading and non-trading) use a company structure to reduce their tax bills by retaining cash within the company to reinvest and grow.

Keeping to this strategy allows only corporation tax to be paid on the profits (and remember corporation tax is generally much lower than income tax). Income tax would only be payable if cash was extracted by the owner.

However, when it comes to share *investment* companies, there is one key issue that could prevent the low tax rates from being exploited.

The Obstacle: Close Investment Companies

Investment companies are subject to different rules from trading companies. Many of the reliefs available to trading companies, such as Entrepreneurs Relief, rollover relief, and business property relief are NOT usually extended to investment companies.

As well as these specific provisions, there are also the Close Investment Company (CIC) provisions which apply to investment companies that are also 'close companies'.

The result of being classed as a CIC is that the lower rates of corporation tax are not available. Instead the company must pay tax at the 28% rate, irrespective of the level of profits.

Therefore, it's very important that we know exactly what a CIC is and when a company will fall within the definition.

What is a Close Investment Company (CIC)?

First of all we must explain what a 'close company' is. In practice almost all small owner-managed companies are 'close companies'. A close company is, generally speaking, any company that is controlled by:

- Its directors (including connected persons).

- Five or fewer participators. 'Participators' are generally shareholders, although this is a potentially wide term and can include loan creditors for a non-commercial loan.

Most companies are controlled by their directors and have fewer than five shareholders.

It's not a problem for a trading company to be classified as a close company. However, close companies that are also *investment* companies are specifically targeted. Just to make matters more confusing, the tax legislation defines a CIC in the negative. A company will be a close investment company *unless* it exists for one or more of the following purposes:

- Carrying on a trade or trades on a commercial basis.

- Making investments in land for letting to unconnected persons.

- Acting as a holding company, in other words holding shares in companies within a trading/property investment group.

- Co-ordinating the administration of two or more group companies involved in trading/property investment activities.

You'll notice that there is a let out for property investment companies... but there is no mercy for share investment companies. It is therefore likely that unless a company dealing in shares can be classed as a *share trading* company, it will be a CIC and pay tax at 28%.

Other Tax Consequences of Using a Company

One of the most important tax consequences of using a company is the loss of the annual capital gains tax exemption – £10,100 in the case of unmarried individuals and £20,200 if you're married and both own investments.

For the very small share investor the loss of this exemption rules out using a company to buy and sell shares – no matter what advantages a company may offer, loss of the annual CGT allowance makes the whole exercise a waste of time.

The second point to note is the extra administrative burden of running a company. The rules governing the preparation of company accounts are stringent so you'll need to employ the services of an accountant – this all eats away at the tax savings you would otherwise have enjoyed.

Thirdly, companies cannot use the 18% rate of CGT that individuals are entitled to.

We now know that the odds are stacked against the use of a company for share *investment* activities due to:

- The CIC provisions
- The loss of the annual CGT exemption
- The loss of 18% CGT rate, and
- The extra admin burden placed on company owners.

As a general rule, share *investment* activities are taxed most favourably when the shares are held personally rather than through a company. It's the CIC provisions that do the real damage, resulting in a massive 28% tax charge before the profits are even extracted. When compared to the 18% rate of CGT that investors pay this is a significant disadvantage. Even if the company is not a CIC you're still better off investing personally and saving yourself at least 3% off the tax rate.

Summary

A company will generally NOT be tax efficient for most share investors.

They will lose the 18% rate of CGT, the annual exemption and will also need to concern themselves with extracting cash from the company (which would also lead to an additional tax charge).

When you also take into account the extra hassle involved most share investors would be mad to use a company for their share investments.

Using an Existing Trading Company

You may already own your own trading company and carry on your share investment activities as a sideline.

It used to be suggested that in these circumstances you could use your existing company to carry out your share dealing. The CIC provisions would only apply if the company exists 'wholly or mainly' for share investment activities during the accounting period.

Now that the rate of CGT has been reduced to below the company tax rate this doesn't stack up.

Furthermore you'd run the risk of the company being reclassified as an investment company. This would be disastrous and could prove costly in tax terms, particularly if the company was sold at a later date.

For Entrepreneurs Relief purposes, HMRC will deny you the 4/9 tax exemption when you sell the company if more than 20% of the company's income or assets are attributable to non-trading activities – you'll therefore need to be careful about the extent of any share investment activities based on the level of the company's income and assets.

Pros and Cons of Offshore Companies

Investors often ask whether they can set up an offshore company (ie, non-UK resident company) to hold assets such as property or shares. What are the tax implications of this?

The first issue is to ascertain whether the company is truly a UK resident or offshore company.

A company is regarded as UK resident if it is either:

- A UK incorporated company, or

- Its central management and control is in the UK.

Central Management and Control (CM&C)

HMRC has stated that it will look at offshore companies to identify if there has been an attempt to create the *appearance* of central management and control, without it actually being exercised in the overseas location.

One common piece of advice is to use overseas directors to control the company. This can be accepted by Revenue and Customs, however it would need to be looked at on a practical level.

Various cases have indicated that if the board of directors meet and give proper consideration to any transactions the company undertakes, such will constitute the central management and control. HMRC may argue that the company is run by the controlling shareholder in the UK. If the overseas directors were simply puppets rubber stamping the UK resident shareholders' decisions, the company would be classed as UK resident.

Therefore, care is needed to ensure that any overseas directors are actually running the company.

In order to pass the CM&C test the majority of the directors should be non-UK resident and the non-UK resident directors should actively participate in making board decisions.

This means that key business decisions should be taken at overseas board meetings. A UK-resident shareholder may therefore establish a non-resident company but the running of the business has to be left to the non-resident directors.

How Are Non-Resident Companies Taxed?

A UK-resident company is subject to UK corporation tax on its *worldwide* income and gains. By contrast a non-UK resident company is only subject to corporation tax on its *UK income* and is exempt from tax on gains from assets sold in the UK or overseas.

These rules are modified for companies that carry on a trade in the UK via a 'branch' or 'agency'. In these circumstances, gains from the sale of assets used in the UK trade are still subject to UK corporation tax.

If the offshore company is regarded as a share investor, any gains realised will be free of UK corporation tax, subject to HMRC tax anti-avoidance provisions discussed below.

Note that if the offshore company is regarded as a share trading company the shares would not be regarded as 'assets' but rather as trading stock. The impact of this would be that any profit on disposal could be treated as income, as opposed to a chargeable gain and, as such, subject to UK corporation tax.

Apportionment of Gains

This, however, is not the end of the matter. HMRC has targeted anti-avoidance legislation to reduce the opportunities for UK residents to use offshore companies to shelter gains.

These anti-avoidance provisions require the gains of a non-resident 'close' company to be apportioned amongst the member shareholders. CGT is levied on those who are resident and, in the case of individuals, domiciled in the UK. As from 6 April 2008 non UK domiciliaries are also brought within the scope of these rules but on an amended basis.

We've already looked at what a close company is, and you'll remember that they include most owner-managed businesses. Therefore a company incorporated overseas, and accepted by HMRC as being non-UK resident, could still have its gains taxed in the UK as a result of these provisions.

There are some significant exceptions to these provisions, such as where the UK-resident shareholders owns less than 10% of the share capital. In this case gains of the offshore company are not attributed to the UK-resident shareholder.

As from 6 April 2008 new provisions introduced in the 2007 Budget mean that UK resident shareholders in overseas companies will be able to claim the 'deemed tax credit' for offset against any UK tax liability.

For the 2008/2009 tax year you would need to own less than 10% of the share capital to qualify. However, provided this was the case it means that the treatment would be similar to the treatment for UK dividends, and basic-rate taxpayers could receive dividends effectively free of UK income tax.

In the 2009 Budget the Chancellor announced that as from 6 April 2009 this 10% shareholding restriction is to be withdrawn providing the overseas company is subject to overseas corporation tax.

Non-resident Shareholders – Dividends

It is possible for an individual to retain cash within the company, then arrange for a dividend to be paid on becoming non-resident. The income tax rules regarding non-residence are more relaxed than the CGT rules. The non-resident shareholder could avoid liability to UK tax on the dividend by ensuring that he is non-resident throughout the relevant tax year of the dividend payment.

A non-resident can receive UK dividends tax free. There is no higher rate liability, and the notional tax credit is regarded as satisfying any basic rate tax liability.

Of course, care must be taken to ensure that the domestic tax legislation of your new country of residence, along with any double tax agreements, do not result in you 'jumping out of the frying pan and into the fire'.

Disposal of Shares in a Personal Company

What about the disposal of shares in the investment company itself?

The disposal of assets, whether UK or overseas, is outside the scope of UK capital gains tax if an individual is non-UK resident, provided that the period of non-residence covers five complete and consecutive tax years and the asset is not used in a UK trading branch/agency.

Example

Phil has been using his personal company, Phil Ltd, to buy and sell shares for investment purposes.

He was non-resident from tax year 2005/2006 and decided to dispose of his shares in Phil Ltd during the 2006/2007 tax year.

As he is non-resident during the tax year in which the disposal takes place, no tax will be payable, provided Phil remains non-UK resident until 6 April 2010.

If Phil were to become UK resident during the 2009/2010 tax year, the gain would be subject to tax in that year.

Note that this treatment only applies to assets held at the date of departure from the UK. Therefore if Phil had acquired further UK shares directly whilst non-resident, these would not be subject to the five-year rule. Provided he was non-resident during the tax year of disposal, these later acquisitions would be exempt from UK capital gains tax.

Non-residence is simply one of the circumstances in which a share investment company can be beneficial. In particular, the extraction of cash as dividends can be a useful mechanism to avoid the onerous CGT provisions. In practical terms it is therefore the shareholder's residence that can offer significant tax-planning opportunities.

Share Trading vs Investment Companies

In Chapter 24 we looked at the pros and cons of being classed as a share trader rather than a share investor. We showed that it is rare that you would benefit from income tax treatment rather than capital gains tax treatment.

In this chapter we have already shown that there is very little benefit to be obtained from setting up a share *investment* company. The CIC provisions will subject the company to the 28% rate of corporation tax irrespective of its profit level, with further income tax payable when profits are extracted.

How about share *trading* companies? Remember, the CIC provisions apply to all close companies except (broadly) those carrying on a trade. Therefore, provided HMRC classes you as a share trader (see Chapter 24 for more information on being classed as a share trader), the CIC provisions will NOT apply and the company's profits will be taxed at much lower rates.

Tax Benefits of Share Trading Companies

The 21% corporation tax rate outlined earlier applies to profits of up to £300,000. For a sole trader, however, profits above £43,875 would be taxed at 40%. With corporation tax rates just over half as high as income tax rates, it's easy to see why companies offer potentially attractive tax savings when profits are reinvested, preferably for many years.

If you want to pay out some of the profits you have a lot of flexibility because you can pay yourself the most tax-efficient mix of salary and dividends. Salaries and dividends are taxed in entirely different ways:

- Salaries are taxed at normal income tax rates (20% or 40% for the current tax year). Dividends are taxed at 0% or an effective 25%.

- Salaries are subject to national insurance (above the lower earnings limit), dividends are not.

- Salaries are tax deductible for the company, dividends are not.

TABLE 6: TRADING VS INVESTMENT
COMPANY VS PERSONAL
Total Tax Bills Compared (£)

Profits	Investor	Trader	CIC Co	Trading Co
10,000	0	1,173	1,200	900
20,000	1,782	3,973	4,000	3,000
30,000	3,582	6,773	6,800	5,100
40,000	5,382	8,798	9,600	7,200
50,000	7,182	13,169	12,400	9,460
60,000	8,982	17,269	16,385	13,535
70,000	10,782	21,369	20,985	17,610
80,000	12,582	25,469	25,585	21,685
90,000	14,382	29,569	30,185	25,760
100,000	16,182	33,669	34,785	29,835
110,000	17,982	37,769	39,385	33,910
120,000	19,782	41,869	43,985	37,985
130,000	21,582	45,969	48,585	42,060
140,000	23,382	50,069	53,185	46,135
150,000	25,182	51,169	57,785	50,210

NOTES:
Investor – Owns shares personally, pays CGT
Trader – Owns shares personally, pays income tax
CIC Co – Company owns shares, pays tax at 28%
Trading Co – Company owns shares, pays tax at normal corporation tax rates

Which option is best will depend on how much other income you earn and the level of the company's profits. However, one route followed by many small business owners is to extract a small tax-free salary, equivalent to the national insurance earnings threshold and the remainder as dividends (tax free if you're a basic-rate taxpayer with no national insurance liability).

So how much tax do you stand to save if you operate a share trading company? Table 6 compares the tax bills at different profit levels of the four categories of investor/trader we've analyzed in this guide. The first column is a share investor who pays capital gains tax on all his profits. The second is a sole trader who pays income tax on all his profits. The third is a share investment company (subject to the CIC provisions and taxed at 28%). Finally column four is the share trading company.

For the companies we've assumed all profits are extracted each year, with a small salary being taken to use up the company owner's national insurance allowance, with the rest taken as dividends. The tax bills for the two company columns are total tax bills taking into account the company's tax and the owner's personal tax.

If you're a share investor (column one) you're still way ahead of the others in terms of paying the lowest taxes. The main advantage of having a share trading company would be if you were otherwise classed as a share trader. In this case there can be some useful tax savings by using a share trading company.

However, in the table we have overstated the tax bill of the share trading company because we have not included any tax-deductible expenditure in the calculation. Remember the private investor cannot deduct any meaningful expenses whereas the share trading company can.

It's easy to see how this will generate further tax savings for the company route. For example, if the share trading company has income of £50,000 but expenses of £10,000, its taxable profits will be £40,000 and the total tax bill will be £7,200 rather than £9,460. This is clearly much lower than the share trader's tax bill of £8,798 and is not much different to the share investor's £7,182!

The problem, of course, is you may have to convince Revenue and Customs that you are a share trading company rather than an investment company. That's why we included column three as a reminder of the potential tax danger. In Table 6 the CIC company has the highest tax bill of all.

We've also ignored the fact that more than one person, eg a spouse, may be involved. If you have a company with two shareholders this would result in more tax savings due to the availability of two personal allowances and two basic-rate tax bands for dividend payments.

There are also capital gains tax benefits to be enjoyed by investors who own shares jointly with their spouses.

TABLE 7: TRADING VS INVESTMENT
COMPANY VS PERSONAL
Total Tax Bills Compared (£) – 2 Persons

Profits	2 Investors	Partnership	CIC Co	Trading Co
10,000	0	250	0	0
20,000	0	2,345	2,400	1,800
30,000	1,764	5,145	5,200	3,900
40,000	3,564	8,945	8,000	6,000
50,000	5,364	10,745	10,800	8,100
60,000	7,164	13,545	13,600	10,200
70,000	8,964	16,345	16,400	12,300
80,000	10,764	17,596	19,200	14,400
90,000	12,564	22,238	22,000	16,500
100,000	14,364	26,338	24,800	18,920
110,000	16,164	30,438	28,170	22,995
120,000	17,964	34,538	32,770	27,070
130,000	19,764	38,638	37,370	31,145
140,000	21,564	42,738	41,970	35,220
150,000	23,364	46,838	46,570	39,295

NOTES:

2 Investors – Own shares personally, pay CGT
Partnership – Own shares personally, pay income tax
CIC Co – Company owns shares, pays tax at 28%
Trading Co – Company owns shares, pays tax at normal corporation tax rates

Table 7 is similar to Table 6, except in each case two persons are involved instead of one.

Being classed as share investors (in other words, being entitled to two annual CGT exemptions) produces the best tax outcome at every profit level. However, this ignores costs. If there are, fairly substantial costs the company route could be more attractive. For example for profits of £100,000 if there were costs of £20,000 the tax bills for holding investments personally or via a trading company are more or less the same.

TABLE 8: COMPANY VS PERSONAL
Tax Bills Compared (£) – 50% Profits Reinvested

Profits	1 Investor	2 Investors	1 Person Co	2 Person Co
10,000	0	0	1,050	0
20,000	1,782	0	3,000	1,800
30,000	3,582	1,764	5,100	3,900
40,000	5,382	3,564	7,200	6,000
50,000	7,182	5,364	9,300	8,100
60,000	8,982	7,164	11,400	10,200
70,000	10,782	8,964	13,664	12,300
80,000	12,582	10,764	17,014	14,400
90,000	14,382	12,564	20,364	16,500
100,000	16,182	14,364	23,714	18,600
110,000	17,982	16,164	27,064	20,700
120,000	19,782	17,964	30,414	22,800
130,000	21,582	19,764	33,764	24,900
140,000	23,382	21,564	37,114	27,328
150,000	25,182	23,364	40,464	30,678

NOTES:

Investors – Owns shares personally, pays CGT
Company – Company owns shares, pays tax at normal corporation tax rates.

So far we've assumed all the profits are extracted from the company. However, one of the main reasons for setting up a company is so that profits can be reinvested without any personal tax being paid, just the low rates of corporation tax.

Table 8 shows the total tax payable by a one- and two-person company with the shareholders extracting 50% of the gross profits by way of a dividend after the payment of a salary equal to the NIC allowance. The remaining 50% is retained within the company to pay corporation tax and reinvest in new share trades (although for profits of £10,000 I've assumed that the salary was reduced to £5,000 to allow the extraction of a £5,000 dividend).

This should settle the argument, and owning investments personally is still likely to be the best option in terms of reducing taxes for most people. There could be scenarios where a two person company would be preferred, for example where there was significant deductible expenditure which will reduce the company's tax bill even further. However as rule this would not be the case.

It's important to note that this is based on particular conditions such as no other income, and the annual exemption being available in full.

In real life, matters are not as straightforward as this, and there are occasions when corporate or individual ownership for both share trading and share investment would be the most beneficial option from a tax perspective.

Share Trading Company – Is it Possible?

The general rule is that it's easier for a company to be classed as a share trader than an individual.

All companies have articles of association and a memorandum of association. These are the internal rule books and are usually standard documents and for most companies, the shareholders will pay little attention to them.

However, it is possible to arrange for customised articles and a memorandum to be drawn up. It would strengthen your case for share trader classification to have these specially drafted.

In particular the memorandum of association often contains a number of paragraphs highlighting the objects of the company. These usually permit the company to carry out all activities of a 'general commercial company'. It would be helpful to show that the memorandum clearly shows the intention to be a share trader.

If there are other share investments contained within the company, the share trading activities would need to be substantial to class the company as a share trader and should be frequent and extend over as long a period as possible.

As with individuals, whether or not share transactions by a company amount to the carrying on of a trade is determined by the particular facts of the case in question, although it is arguably less difficult for a company to be held to be a financial trader than an individual. Ultimately, if the taxpayer and HMRC cannot come to an agreement, it may be necessary to appeal to the Commissioners of the Inland Revenue to determine the matter.

It is impossible to simply set out 'rules' to be followed to obtain or not obtain share trader status. These are covered in detail in Chapter 24 and they are all relevant to sole traders AND companies. In order to be classed as a trader, it would be expected that a trading activity should be organized in a professional manner. This ties in with all the other factors and is to a large extent the thread that underlies them all.

Take Peter, for example. Let's say he has a home office and spends five hours each day trading shares using a variety of sophisticated strategies. His portfolio is worth approximately £500,000 and this is his sole occupation.

In my opinion, there would be a case that Peter was a share trader – his activities have the appearance of a trade.

If Peter operated through a company, Peter's Trading Limited, in which he manages his own funds and those of other family members, it would be difficult to argue against the company being classed as a share trader. By showing a 'deliberate and organized scheme of profit making' you are increasing the chances of the Revenue arguing you are a share trader.

However, it's essential that you receive professional advice before setting up any company to trade shares.

Summary

As with all major decisions, there is no straightforward answer and the decision to engage in share dealing activities via a company would need to be carefully considered. Share investors are generally better off investing personally.

Chapter 26

How Share Clubs are Taxed

Share clubs are becoming increasingly popular. Essentially what happens is a group of friends or colleagues put some cash in a 'pot' and this is then used to invest in shares that the group vote on. At predetermined intervals the profit is distributed to the members.

It's a good way to make stock market investments with a lower initial sum, and allows a sharing of risks and rewards, with a wider spread of knowledge and experience.

There is a special entity available for share clubs, known as an 'investment club'. Investment clubs are pretty common and are a recognised structure through which individuals can each invest cash for a common investment fund. Under current taxation legislation, most forms of unincorporated associations pay corporation tax on their profits, even though they are not actually companies.

However, investment clubs are different. The income an investment club makes from its investments is regarded as the members' income and the club is treated as a 'pass-through' entity for tax purposes. This means the club itself receives the income in a representative capacity which excludes it from the requirement to pay corporation tax.

As the club itself only acts as a representative of the members, it is treated for tax purposes like a partnership, with each member of the club being charged to tax on the profits of the club. For a normal share dealing investment club, the members would be subject to income tax on any dividends received and capital gains tax on profits when shares are sold.

Each club member would therefore need to declare their apportioned share of dividends or gains received from investments made by the club on the self assessment tax return. The club treasurer should provide an annual statement of the gains and losses on the club investments so in practice the filing should be very straightforward.

The general rules still apply so a member of a share club does not need to declare his share of investment club gains to the taxman if:

- Those gains, together with any other gains, are less than the annual exemption (currently £10,100) and

- His or her share of the proceeds from all disposals in the tax year is less than four times the annual exemption (currently £40,400).

As the share investment club is a 'pass through' entity the members are automatically charged to income tax or capital gains tax when the income and gains arise. It therefore makes no difference to the member's tax liability whether cash is extracted by the members or retained within the club.

Spread Betting Investment Clubs

If the club's activity is spread betting, which is treated for tax purposes as 'gambling', it is exempt from capital gains tax and stamp duty. Income tax is only levied if the activity was to be considered a trade.

As the Revenue do not normally regard gambling as a trading activity the individual members of the club would not be taxed on their share of the annual income/profits of the investment club, if they are regarded as carrying on the activity of spread betting. This is just an alignment with the treatment of individuals undertaking spread betting.

Tax Rates and Allowances
2007/2008 to 2009/2010

	Rates	Bands, Allowances, etc.		
		2007/2008 £	2008/2009 £	2009/2010 £
Income tax				
Personal allowance		5,225	6,035	6,475
Starting rate	10%	2,230	-	-
Basic rate	22%/20%*	32,370	34,800	37,400
Higher rate on over	40%	34,600	34,800	37,400

*Basic rate is 20% for tax year 2008/2009 onwards

	2007/2008 £	2008/2009 £	2009/2010 £
Capital Gains Tax			
Annual exemption:			
Individuals	9,200	9,600	10,100
Trusts	4,600	4,800	5,050
Inheritance Tax			
Nil Rate Band Threshold	300,000	312,000	325,000
Pensioners, etc.			
Age allowance: 65 –74	7,550	9,030	9,490
Age allowance: 75 & over	7,690	9,180	9,640
MCA: born before 6/4/35	6,285	6,535	-
MCA: 75 & over	6,365	6,625	6,965
MCA minimum	2,440	2,540	2,670
Income limit	20,900	21,800	22,900
Blind Person's Allowance	1,730	1,800	1,890

Appendix B

Indexation Relief Rates

Percentages applying to disposals made after April 5 1998

Month of Acquisition	Rate %	Month of Acquisition	Rate %
March 1982 or earlier	104.7	July 1985	70.7
April 1982	100.6	August 1985	70.3
May 1982	99.2	September 1985	70.4
June 1982	98.7	October 1985	70.1
July 1982	98.6	November 1985	69.5
August 1982	98.5	December 1985	69.3
September 1982	98.7	January 1986	68.9
October 1982	97.7	February 1986	68.3
November 1982	96.7	March 1986	68.1
December 1982	97.1	April 1986	66.5
January 1983	96.8	May 1986	66.2
February 1983	96.0	June 1986	66.3
March 1983	95.6	July 1986	66.7
April 1983	92.9	August 1986	67.1
May 1983	92.1	September 1986	65.4
June 1983	91.7	October 1986	65.2
July 1983	90.6	November 1986	63.8
August 1983	89.8	December 1986	63.2
September 1983	88.9	January 1987	62.6
October 1983	88.3	February 1987	62.0
November 1983	87.6	March 1987	61.6
December 1983	87.1	April 1987	59.7
January 1984	87.2	May 1987	59.6
February 1984	86.5	June 1987	59.6
March 1984	85.9	July 1987	59.7
April 1984	83.4	August 1987	59.3
May 1984	82.8	September 1987	58.8
June 1984	82.3	October 1987	58.0
July 1984	82.5	November 1987	57.3
August 1984	80.8	December 1987	57.4
September 1984	80.4	January 1988	57.4
October 1984	79.3	February 1988	56.8
November 1984	78.8	March 1988	56.2
December 1984	78.9	April 1988	54.5
January 1985	78.3	May 1988	53.1
February 1985	76.9	June 1988	52.5
March 1985	75.2	July 1988	52.4
April 1985	71.6	August 1988	50.7
May 1985	70.8	September 1988	50.0
June 1985	70.4	October 1988	48.5

Appendix B (contd)

Month of Acquisition	Rate %	Month of Acquisition	Rate %
November 1988	47.8	September 1992 16.6	
December 1988	47.4	October 1992	16.2
January 1989	46.5	November 1992	16.4
February 1989	45.4	December 1992	16.8
March 1989	44.8	January 1993	17.9
April 1989	42.3	February 1993	17.1
May 1989	41.4	March 1993	16.7
June 1989	40.9	April 1993	15.6
July 1989	40.8	May 1993	15.2
August 1989	40.4	June 1993	15.3
September 1989	39.5	July 1993	15.6
October 1989	38.4	August 1993	15.1
November 1989	37.2	September 1993	14.6
December 1989	36.9	October 1993	14.7
January 1990	36.1	November 1993	14.8
February 1990	35.3	December 1993	14.6
March 1990	33.9	January 1994	15.1
April 1990	30.0	February 1994	14.4
May 1990	28.8	March 1994	14.1
June 1990	28.3	April 1994	12.8
July 1990	28.2	May 1994	12.4
August 1990	26.9	June 1994	12.4
September 1990	25.8	July 1994	12.9
October 1990	24.8	August 1994	12.4
November 1990	25.1	September 1994	12.1
December 1990	25.2	October 1994	12.0
January 1991	24.9	November 1994	11.9
February 1991	24.2	December 1994	11.4
March 1991	23.7	January 1995	11.4
April 1991	22.2	February 1995	10.7
May 1991	21.8	March 1995	10.2
June 1991	21.3	April 1995	9.1
July 1991	21.5	May 1995	8.7
August 1991	21.3	June 1995	8.5
September 1991	20.8	July 1995	9.1
October 1991	20.4	August 1995	8.5
November 1991	19.9	September 1995	8.0
December 1991	19.8	October 1995	8.5
January 1992	19.9	November 1995	8.5
February 1992	19.3	December 1995	7.9
March 1992	18.9	January 1996	8.3
April 1992	17.1	February 1996	7.8
May 1992	16.7	March 1996	7.3
June 1992	16.7	April 1996	6.6
July 1992	17.1	May 1996	6.3
August 1992	17.1	June 1996	6.3

Appendix B (contd)

Month of Acquisition	Rate %
July 1996	6.7
August 1996	6.2
September 1996	5.7
October 1996	5.7
November 1996	5.7
December 1996	5.3
January 1997	5.3
February 1997	4.9
March 1997	4.6
April 1997	4.0
May 1997	3.6
June 1997	3.2
July 1997	3.2
August 1997	2.6
September 1997	2.1
October 1997	1.9
November 1997	1.9
December 1997	1.6
January 1998	1.9
February 1998	1.4
March 1998	1.1
April 1998 or later	0.0

Pay Less Tax!

...with help from Taxcafe's unique tax guides and software

All products available online at **www.taxcafe.co.uk/books**

How to Avoid Property Tax
By Carl Bayley BSc ACA

How to Avoid Property Tax is widely regarded as *the* tax bible for property investors. This unique and bestselling guide is jam packed with ideas that will save you thousands in income tax and capital gains tax.

"A valuable guide to the tax issues facing buy-to-let investors" - **THE INDEPENDENT**

How to Avoid Tax on Foreign Property
By Carl Bayley BSc ACA

Find out everything you need to know about paying less tax on overseas property. Completely up to date with key UK and overseas tax changes.

Using a Property Company to Save Tax
By Carl Bayley

Currently a 'hot topic' for the serious property investor, this guide shows how you can significantly boost your after-tax returns by setting up your own property company and explains ALL the tax consequences of property company ownership.

"An excellent tax resource....informative and clearly written" **The Letting Update Journal**

Keeping It Simple
By James Smith BSc ACA

This plain-English guide tells you everything you need to know about small business bookkeeping, accounting, tax returns and VAT.

Property Capital Gains Tax Calculator
By Carl Bayley

This powerful piece of software will calculate in seconds the capital gains tax payable when you sell a property and help you cut the tax bill. It provides tax planning tips based on your personal circumstances and a concise summary and detailed breakdown of all calculations.

Tax-Free Property Investments
By Nick Braun PhD

This guide shows you how to double your investment returns using a variety of powerful tax shelters. You'll discover how to buy property at a 40% discount, paid for by the taxman, never pay tax on your property profits again and invest tax free in overseas property.

The World's Best Tax Havens
By Lee Hadnum

This book provides a fascinating insight into the glamorous world of tax havens and how you can use them to cut your taxes to zero and safeguard your financial freedom.

How to Avoid Inheritance Tax
By Carl Bayley

Making sure you adequately plan for inheritance tax could save you literally hundreds of thousands of pounds. *How to Avoid Inheritance Tax* is a unique guide which will tell you all you need to know about sheltering your family's money from the taxman. This guide is essential reading for parents, grandparents and adult children.

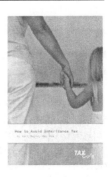

"Useful source of Inheritance Tax information" **What Investment Magazine**

Using a Company to Save Tax
By Lee Hadnum

By running your business through a limited company you stand to save tens of thousands of pounds in tax and national insurance every year. This tax guide tells you everything you need to know about the tax benefits of incorporation.

Salary versus Dividends
By Carl Bayley

This unique guide is essential reading for anyone running their business as a limited company. After reading it, you will know the most tax efficient way in which to extract funds from your company, and save thousands in tax!

Selling Your Business
By Lee Hadnum

This guide tells you everything you need to know about paying less tax and maximizing your profits when you sell your business. It is essential reading for anyone selling a company or sole trader business.

How to Avoid Tax on Stock Market Profits
By Lee Hadnum

This tax guide can only be described as THE definitive tax-saving resource for stock market investors and traders. Anyone who owns shares, unit trusts, ISAs, corporate bonds or other financial assets should read it as it contains a huge amount of unique tax planning information.

Non-Resident & Offshore Tax Planning
By Lee Hadnum LLB ACA CTA

By becoming non-resident or moving your assets offshore it is possible to cut your tax bill to zero. This guide explains what you have to do and all the traps to avoid. Also contains detailed info on using offshore trusts and companies.

"The ultimate guide to legal tax avoidance" **Shelter Offshore**

How to Profit from Off-Plan Property
By Alyssa and David Savage

This property investment guide tells you everything you need to know about investing in off-plan and new-build property. It contains a fascinating insight into how you can make big money from off-plan property... and avoid all the pitfalls along the way.

Lightning Source UK Ltd.
Milton Keynes UK
10 December 2009

147341UK00001B/12/P